VIA DOLOROSA

A Contemplative Journey to Calvary

by E. Mary Christie

First printing February 2011
© 2011 E. Mary Christie
All rights reserved.

The content of this book is the personal revelation of the author and is shared with the intent to acquaint the reader with Our Lord and Saviour, Jesus Christ through that revelation. Professional spiritual direction is neither intended nor implied.

Scriptural references taken from the Latin Vulgate Douay-Rheims Catholic Bible (Biblia Scara Vulgata) (translated from the original Greek/Hebrew texts into Latin by Saint Jerome and confirmed by Pope Pius XII in his 1943 encyclical letter, Divino Afflante Spiritu, to be 'free from any error whatsoever in matters of faith and morals').

Published by
Mother's House Publishing
2814 East Woodmen Road
Colorado Springs, CO 80920
719-266-0437 / 800-266-0999
info@mothershousepublishing.com
www.mothershousepublishing.com

Printed and bound in Colorado Springs, CO
Made in the United States of America

ISBN 978-1-935086-96-3

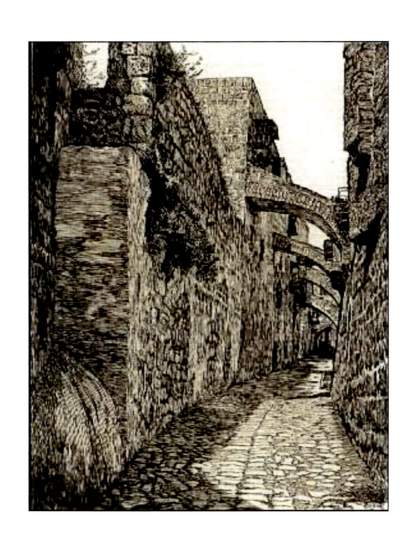

Stairway to Calvary, located on the right just inside the entrance to the Church of the Holy Sepulchre, Jerusalem

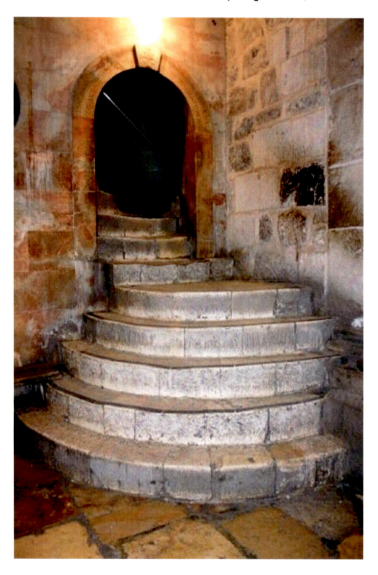

Photo of the Facade and Courtyard of The Church of the Holy Sepulchre from the 1890s

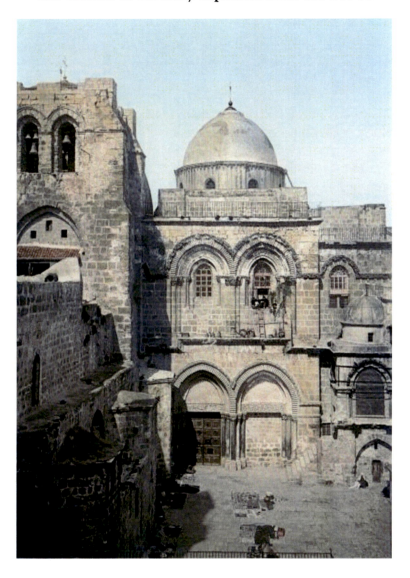

Saint Jerome:

St. Jerome (342-420) was one of the four great Western Fathers of the Church—a man believed to have been inspired by God to translate the Holy Bible into the common Latin tongue of his day. He knew Latin and Greek perfectly; his translation is acknowledged as a careful, word-for-word rendering of the original texts into Latin. He was 1,500 years closer to the original languages than any scholar today, which made him a better judge of the exact meaning of any Greek or Hebrew word in the Scriptures; he had access to ancient Hebrew and Greek manuscripts of the Second and Third Centuries which have since perished and are no longer available to scholars. Besides being a linguistic genius, he was also a great saint.

TABLE OF CONTENTS

FIRST STATION OF THE CROSS 1

SECOND STATION OF THE CROSS 10

THIRD STATION OF THE CROSS 16

FOURTH STATION OF THE CROSS 20

FIFTH STATION OF THE CROSS 26

SIXTH STATION OF THE CROSS 31

SEVENTH STATION OF THE CROSS 37

EIGHTH STATION OF THE CROSS 42

NINTH STATION OF THE CROSS 47

TENTH STATION OF THE CROSS 51

ELEVENTH STATION OF THE CROSS 59

TWELFTH STATION OF THE CROSS 65

THIRTEENTH STATION OF THE CROSS 79

FOURTEENTH STATION OF THE CROSS 87

Dear Reader,

Meditating on the stations along the *Via Dolorosa*, the Way of the Cross, is as old as Christianity itself. It first dates back to the Blessed Virgin Mary, Mother of Jesus Christ, who, Tradition reveals, had a habit of visiting those places in Jerusalem where her beloved Son suffered throughout His Passion. She would then take the narrow street leading out of the city and up the Hill of Golgotha, otherwise known as Calvary, thus to tread the rugged highway along which Christ carried His Cross to His Crucifixion and Death. No doubt, in the peaceful quietude of the early morn before the hustle and bustle of early risers, she would take time to pause along the Way, shed her tears upon the ground that His Most Precious Blood had soaked or upon which His Sacred Body had fallen, and pray, feeling the Presence of her Divine Son as one at the graveside of a dearly beloved.

Inspired by the Holy Gospels and by the revelations of various well-known Saints, the author invites you to step back in time through the book's vivid portrayal of the Passion, Crucifixion, and Death of our loving Lord and Saviour - thereby drawing you to a deeper and more meaningful contemplation of His sufferings along the *Via Dolorosa* (devoutly practised as the Fourteen Stations of the Cross by Christians throughout the world these past many centuries).

As you courageously follow Christ's bloody Footsteps from the time of His unjust sentencing by Pilate to His Crucifixion, Death, and Burial on Calvary, may this Contemplative Journey ignite your imagination in a way that enhances your love, respect and worship of our Redeemer. May it open your heart to an undying gratitude for the terrible sufferings Jesus endured out of His immeasurably merciful love for us in saving our souls and re-opening for us the Gates of Heaven - thereby strengthening your resolve to never again offend His Infinite Goodness.

E. Mary Christie

CHRIST PRESENTED TO THE PEOPLE
Pilate saith unto them, Shall I crucify your King?   (John 19:15)

FIRST STATION OF THE CROSS
Jesus is Condemned to Death
Moral Courage

Good Friday. A day of solemn rejoicing in that Christ died to save our souls, thus breaking the barrier of sin to re-open for us the Gates of Heaven.

Yet in the bright sunshine of that early Friday morn,[1] it is difficult for our hearts to feel gladdened as we contemplate the Man standing before Pontius Pilate:[2] our Lord and Saviour, Jesus Christ—Sacrificial Lamb of God—battered, bruised, beaten, scourged, scorned and violated.[3]

In abject horror, we visualize His Divine Countenance, bruised, slashed and bleeding, His eyes dark-ringed and bloodshot, His lips cut and swollen. A woven chaplet of twisted thorn branches crowns His sacred head, His hair and beard already soaked from the steady flow of blood as the cruel thorns drive their way into His scalp. We note His loosely-hanging mantle, bloodstained and dirty, exposing savage lacerations across His shoulders, back and arms. His bloodied hands and feet are manacled with a coarse heavy rope[4] already saturated and dripping. His body is hunched over, every muscle quivering

---

[1] Matt. 27:1; Mark 15:1
[2] Roman procurator of Judaea, 26-36AD
[3] John 19:5
[4] Matt. 27:2; Mark 15:1

Jesus is Condemned to Death
Moral Courage

---

from excruciating pain.

We choke back sobs of mortification. Can the atoning punishment for our despicable sinfulness truly warrant such torturous agony?

Yet, silent and resolute He stands upon the platform, Jesus Christ, our Redeemer.

A hush has settled over the ugly crowd gathered in and around the courtyard of the Prætorium—an electrifying silence, like the calm before an outrageous storm—the blackened clouds of hatred, envy, rage and fear gathered for outburst, awaiting the final sentencing of Pilate as he sits upon his Seat of Judgment.[5]

Hundreds of soldiers are stationed around the Prætorium for fear of another insurrection such as had taken place the year before at the Paschal time, the sun glistening off their metal shields and breastplates, blinding in their compacted assembly. Atop the stone walls of the forum is a tightly packed line of archers, their arrows drawn at the ready; every trained eye anxiously searching the mob for the first sign of outbreak. A vicious mob of the most vile and iniquitous of miscreants: hooligans, roughians and pagans, rounded up by those of the

---

[5] John 19:13

Jesus is Condemned to Death
Moral Courage

Pharisees,[6] Sadducees,[7] chief priests, ancients (elders) and scribes who feared and opposed Jesus[8] and had insidiously incited the crowd to violence.

    Crouched near the entrance of Pilate's enclosed arena is the Blessed Virgin Mary, Mother of Jesus—her face, pale and tear-stained, her eyes red-rimmed from weeping. Anxiety, dread and a terrifying fear for her Son engulf her lovely countenance. From a distance she has already witnessed the savage scourging[9] Jesus received at the hands of some four or more brutal torturers, who had massacred His body with continuous lashings, using multi-tailed knotted whips of the most barbarous design, with steel balls, barbs of wire or bits of glass tied to the ends; inebriated, mocking grins fixed to their cruel, blood-spattered faces as they flailed their Victim mercilessly, ignoring the chunks of flesh being ripped from His shuddering body. At her side are John, the apostle Jesus loves as a close brother, and Mary Magdalen (devoted disciple whom Jesus had healed of seven devils[10]), there to support the gentle Virgin but themselves clearly distressed, crushed and devastated.

---

[6] Separatists, or extremists of Judaism, first appearing in 2BC; they sought to give complete obedience to every precept of the oral and written Mosaic law, The Torah [M.C. Tenney]. After the destruction of the Second Temple, the Pharisaic sect was re-established as Rabbinic Judaism - which ultimately produced normative, traditional Judaism.

[7] Members of a priestly, aristocratic Jewish sect. Founded in 2BC, they ceased to exist after the destruction of Herod's Temple in 70AD.

[8] Matt. 12:14; Matt. 16:21, 20:18; 26:4; Luke 7:32; John 11:53, 56

[9] John 19:1

[10] Luke 8:2

Jesus is Condemned to Death
Moral Courage

In the momentary dread-filled silence, Pilate's voice, high-pitched and scathing, heralds an unexpected announcement: *"Behold, I bring Him forth unto you, that you may know that I find no cause in Him"*.[11] A prompt wild scream breaks forth from the riled miscreants, *"Crucify Him! Crucify Him!"*[12]

With abject loathing, Pilate surveys the enraged mob.

Earlier, to appease their wild demands, he had released Barabbas, a notorious murderer, over Jesus,[13] in spite of the warning from his wife that she had had a dream and had beseeched Pilate to have no part in condemning *that just Man.*[14] Her words swarm again through his head; fear and uncertainty unsettling him further. He mulls over the earlier conversation he had had with Jesus when he had asked of Him: *"Art thou a king then?"*[15] to which Jesus had responded: *"Thou sayest it. For this was I born, and for this came I into the world; that I should give testimony to the Truth. Every one that is of the Truth, heareth My voice"*.[16]

Much troubled, Pilate now addresses the sea of faces amassed below his platform, *"Take Him yourselves and crucify*

---

[11] John 19:4; Luke 23:4
[12] Luke 23:21; John 19:6; Mark 15:13-14
[13] Mark 15:6-8; Luke 23:17-20; John 18:40
[14] Matt. 27:19
[15] John 18:37
[16] John 18:37

Jesus is Condemned to Death
Moral Courage

Him, for I find no cause in Him".[17]

Alas, a shrill voice causes him to pause: "*We have a law; and* according *to the law he ought to die, because he made himself the Son of God*".[18]

Disturbed anew, Pilate leaves his Seat of Judgment momentarily to take Jesus aside, now demanding of Him, "*From whence art thou?*"[19] But the Sacrificial Lamb of God makes no reply. "*Speakest thou not to me?*" Pilate insists. "*Knowest thou not that I have the power to crucify thee, and the power to release thee?*"[20] Lifting His thorn-crowned head, the Son of God then gently responds, "*Thou shouldst not have any power over Me, unless it were given thee from Above. Therefore, he that hath delivered Me to thee, hath the greater sin.*"[21]

Returning to his Seat of Judgment, Pilate cautiously surveys the unruly mob before him, fear and cowardice now turmoiling within him. It being the day before the Paschal Sabbath (the Parasceve of the Pasch)[22] in fact the eve of a High Sabbath falling within the Paschal Week,[23] already he had heard

---

[17] Luke 23:22
[18] John 19:7
[19] John 19:9
[20] John 19:10
[21] John 19:11
[22] John 19:14. The Parasceve, the day before the Paschal Sabbath. The eve of every Sabbath was called the Parasceve, or day of preparation.
[23] John 19:31

Jesus is Condemned to Death
Moral Courage

menacing accusations that he was disrupting the Festival and that the high priests would complain to the Emperor against him, demanding that he make up his mind at once as they were obliged to be in the Temple that night.

A piercing voice breaks through the demented shrieking, *"If thou release this man, thou art no friend of Caesar. For whosoever maketh himself a king, speaketh against Caesar"*.[24] A deathly hush falls over the mob.

Suspense builds in the heat of the early morning sun.

With an effort to appear calm, Pilate waves his hand deprecatingly toward Jesus: *"Behold your king!"*[25] he announces. But the crowd screams all the louder, *"Away with him! Crucify him!"*[26]

"Shall I crucify your king?"[27] the troubled Pilate demands. The Sadducees loudly respond: *"We have no king but Caesar"*.[28] At these words, the tempo of the mob escalates into a wild frenzy; their yells and imprecations by now deafening, ringing out from every corner of the forum and beyond.

Fearing another insurrection, Pilate then reluctantly determines to ignore the voice of his own conscience in favour

---

[24] John 19:12
[25] John 19:14
[26] John 19:15
[27] John 19:15
[28] John 19:15

Jesus is Condemned to Death
Moral Courage

---

of surrendering to the demon forces – cowardice overriding the fearful warnings swirling through his mind.

His eyes furtively scan the soldiers standing at the ready, their hearts cold and dispassionate.

He silences the raucousness with the sound of his trumpet.

Inwardly trembling from the impact of what he feels compelled to do, Pilate then delivers his damning sentence, condemning *Jesus of Nazareth, King of the Jews,*[29] to be crucified.

No words can describe the chilling toll of that iniquitous death knell as we contemplate the fate of our beloved Lord and Saviour—already savagely tortured beyond human endurance.

In silent dread, we again visualize His Divine Countenance: His eyes cast downward as He humbly accepts the sentencing, determined as He is to accomplish the holy Will of the Eternal Father—thus to become the new sacrificial Pascal Lamb at this Feast of the Passover, thereby replacing the old covenant God made with Abraham with the new and eternal covenant through the sacrificial outpouring of His own blood to atone for our wretched sinfulness.[30]

Instinctively our thoughts turn to His gentle Mother, the

---

[29] Matt.27:11; Mark 15:2; Mark 15:9

Jesus is Condemned to Death
Moral Courage

Blessed Virgin Mary. We picture her collapsed in the arms of John, the chilling horror of Pilate's sentencing engulfing her consciousness.

We reflect upon the times we ourselves, like Pilate, have ignored the voice of moral reason in favour of surrendering to the voice of cowardice. O Most Sacred Heart of Jesus, we pray: Grant us the gift of Moral Courage in the face of such temptation.

*We adore Thee, O Christ, and we praise Thee
Because by Thy holy Cross Thou hast redeemed the world.*

---

[30] Heb.9:11-15

The Inscription on the Cross

SECOND STATION OF THE CROSS
Jesus Takes Up His Cross
Patience

Pilate's sentencing occurs within the Third Hour[1] of that Friday morning. In biblical times, the twelve hour day commenced at sunrise (6:00 am) and ended at sunset (6:00 pm), the day being divided into four three-hourly parts, named as of the hour from which they began: the First Hour being 6:00 am to 9:00 am; the Third Hour, 9:00 am to Noon; the Sixth Hour, Noon to 3:00 pm; the Ninth Hour, 3:00 pm to 6:00 pm.

Swiftly following the Procurator's announcement, the Roman guards move in, surrounding Jesus. Mocking Him with loud jeers, they savagely tear off the purple mantle thrown over His nakedness during their contemptible ceremony of the crowning of thorns,[2] the garment by this time adhered to His lacerated back and arms after the earlier vicious scourging when chunks of His sacred flesh had been strewn around the courtyard. We cringe as the savage divestment painfully rips open those gaping wounds to set the flow of blood coursing down our Saviour's body with renewed voluminosity.

The guards appear impervious to the excruciating effect of their violent treatment; the body of their Victim now shaking

---

[1] Mark 15:25
[2] Matt. 27:31; Mark 15:17; John 19:2

Jesus Takes Up His Cross
Patience

---

uncontrollably from shock and inexorable pain. They continue to mock Jesus as they cut away the coarse twine binding His hands and feet, and then proceed to make fun of Him as He struggles to put on His own garments[3] and the seamless robe lovingly woven for Him by His Mother. In spite of their sacrilegious taunts, the Sacrificial Lamb of God remains meek and silent.

Roman soldiers on horseback gallop up, dragging behind them a heavy wooden crossbeam by means of stout ropes attached to their team of horses. In gaping horror we envision Jesus, already savagely scourged, battered, bruised and beaten, forced to raise the patibulum (some hundred pounds in weight) from its position on the ground, the soldiers flailing Him with whips as they impatiently goad Him into action, shouting abuse at Him all the while.

Even as Jesus links His arms around its weighty thickness, we wince as the splinters from the coarse grain become embedded into His hands, already cut and bleeding. Yet does the Son of God continue to embrace the wood of the Cross[4] for our sake, even (as some Saints have revealed) to the point of kissing it, knowing it will lead to our Salvation.

---

[3] Matt. 27:31; Mark 15:20

[4] Typically, though sometimes depicted otherwise in Christian art, the upright (*stipes/stirpes*) of the Cross remained at the place of execution, and the crossbeam (*patibulum*) was carried across the shoulders of the prisoner to the execution site. [*Wikipedia Encyclopedia*]

Jesus Takes Up His Cross
Patience

Desperately Jesus now struggles to raise the crossbeam to shoulder height. Weakened from thirst, hunger, a voluminous loss of blood and from being tortured throughout the night, His trembling knees buckle under its hideous weight.

Hurling insults, the guards twist ropes around His waist, pitilessly crushing His lacerations, and bind His arms to the crossbeam. They then proceed to pull on the rope-ends by way of savage assistance, oblivious to anything but their impatience to have the Prisoner get started on the walk to His execution on Calvary's hilltop (otherwise known as Golgotha, Place of the Skull).[5]

In sadness we contemplate the arduous journey ahead of Jesus. Bowed under the cumbersome crossbeam, His faltering Footsteps must first negotiate the narrow streets of Jerusalem, many of them paved with cobblestones. His feet bear no sandals or other footwear; we can only imagine the painful stubbing of His toes against their uneven surface as He shuffles under the weight of that cruel burden. Even worse, once outside the city, the climb to Golgotha is a rugged and steep one, the rough ground fraught with pitfalls and sharp stones of varying shapes and sizes. Adding to that nightmare is the heat of the overhead morning sun, already a blistering ball in the cloudless blue skies; a further challenge to both exhaust and dehydrate the Son of Man.

In choking horror, we contemplate our beloved Saviour

---

[5] Matt. 27:33; Mark 15:22; John 19:17

Jesus Takes Up His Cross
Patience

---

as He staggers painfully forward, step by slow step, His back buckled under the grievous weight of the crossbeam which straddles His torn and bleeding shoulders, His hands dangling motionless with both wrists now bound to the beam. Powerless to control its swaying motion, Jesus fights to maintain His balance. All the while, guards and soldiers alike continue to deride Him and to yank upon the rope-ends, even cracking their whips over His back in their obsession to make the Prisoner move more quickly. All about them the air is filled with the screams of demented souls.

Accompanying the procession walks a man carrying a wooden plaque being the inscription *"Jesus of Nazareth, King of the Jews,"*[6] the scathing cause of death that Pilate had written, deliberately adding the word Nazareth—it being the Prisoner's small hometown of no significance and generally scorned. As we hear the words of Nathanael, quoted in Biblical Scriptures, *"Can any thing of good come from Nazareth?"*[7]

By now a number of the miscreants, appeased by Pilate's lethal verdict, have pushed ahead in their shameless urge to station themselves along the street and thus catch sight of the Man they sought to crucify as He staggers toward His place of execution.

Even within the streets of Jerusalem, as Jesus struggles painfully over the uneven paving, other inhabitants turn to

---
[6] John 19:19
[7] John 1:46

Jesus Takes Up His Cross
Patience

---

survey the procession. Many are pitiless over the fate of the brutalized Victim, yelling their own abuses and obscenities, some throwing stones or items of garbage at Jesus—others even spitting at Him. Each of them ignorant that they are reviling Divinity, God's only Begotten Son made Man, magnanimously offering Himself in sacrifice to the Eternal Father to atone for their (and our) wretched sinfulness.

In the meantime, our meditation again seeks out the Blessed Virgin Mary, Mother of the Word Incarnate; her soul surely fragmented by the sword of Simeon's prophecy, *"Thy own soul a sword shall pierce, that out of many hearts, thoughts may be revealed"*.[8] John and Mary Magdalen's efforts to keep her away from the vicious crowd are in vain—her motherly heart is stubbornly determined to stay with her Son, to be there for Him no matter how severely the grievous pain would crush her. Unable to break through the oncoming mob of unruly miscreants or the solid barrier of soldiers, we can imagine them stepping back into the protection of a stony alcove to await a suitable gap in the crowd before continuing their struggle to reach Jesus.

Inevitably the Son of God, knowing all things, is comforted by their efforts. He patiently struggles on, bearing the full weight of the crossbeam across His lacerated shoulders—the swaying motion gnawing away at the open gashes to expose naked bone.

---

[8] Luke 2:35

Jesus Takes Up His Cross
Patience

O Most Sacred Heart of Jesus, we pray: Grant us the gift of Patience that we may take up our own crosses, so small and insignificant in comparison to what Thou bore for us—to bear all our trials and sorrows tolerantly and with humility, without bitterness or complaint—in loving gratitude to Thee, our Divine Redeemer.

We adore Thee, O Christ, and we praise Thee
Because by Thy holy Cross Thou hast redeemed the world.

THIRD STATION OF THE CROSS
Jesus Falls for the First Time
Strength

Still in the narrow streets of Jerusalem, our meditation seeks out Jesus. He is doggedly bearing the weight of His holy Cross; in His humanity quietly praying to the Eternal Father for strength to continue His redemptive journey.

The robe, lovingly woven for Him by His Mother, is now ripped from savage handling and hangs loosely over His staggering frame, its hem dragging over the cobbled paving to catch under His faltering Footsteps, causing Him to stumble constantly. His cruel tormenters promptly seize each such opportunity to yank and pull on the rope-ends in their shameless effort to keep Jesus upright and moving forward; the see-sawed effect of the swaying crossbeam continuing to aggravate His ugly shoulder wounds. Already His sacred body is leaving a trail of blood—the persistent jerking on the rope-ends re-opening the lacerations across His torso, causing a fresh flow to drip over the cobblestones beneath His bleeding feet.

In agonized dismay, we continue to visualize the Divine Countenance of Christ. His swollen eyelids are fluttering in excruciating agony as He shuffles painfully forward. We note His one eye is almost sealed shut from an open wound stretching across the eyebrow, its weeping flow enjoining that from the ring of barbarous thorns. His Most Precious Blood

Jesus Falls for the First Time
Strength

---

glistens in the brilliant sunshine as it continues to soak His hair and runs down into His beard; both already matting from its steady coagulation in the heat of the morning sun.

We meditatively follow Christ's bloody Footsteps, dreading His first heavy fall at this Third Station along the *Way of the Cross*.

We contemplate the nature of the narrow cobbled street at this Third Station. It is said that a subterranean aqueduct proceeding from Mount Sion passed under the *Via Dolorosa* at this point, wherein lay a hollow often filled with muddy water. A large stone had been placed over its centre to assist travellers negotiating the difficult spot.[1] Like one in the grip of a nightmare we now foresee the danger ahead for our beloved Saviour.

Suffering from extreme exhaustion and struggling to maintain His balance under the weight of the swaying crossbeam, Jesus meets the stony divide, unable to lift His feet sufficiently to cross over the narrow mud-filled gap. Devoid of compassion, His captors lash out with their whips, as the impatient rider of a donkey might flail his charge.

Forced to take a larger step and missing the stone entirely, Jesus falls—crashing to His knees in the slippery mud and hitting His head against the stony divide. With the impact

---

[1] From the visions of Blessed Anne Emmerich, Augustinian nun, stigmatic, mystic, visionary, ecstatic. Sept. 8, 1774 - Feb. 9, 1824.

Jesus Falls for the First Time
Strength

---

of the fall, the crown of thorns becomes further impaled into His skull, its razor-sharp needle-points lethally piercing the tender area across His brow and promptly staining the mud with a renewed flow of blood.

Time stands still in a capsule of abject horror as we meditatively survey the scene. His hands helplessly bound to the crossbeam, Jesus remains face down in the soggy mire—the full weight of the Cross pinning Him down.

His abrupt fall brings the procession to a grinding halt. No helping hand reaches out to our beloved Lord. No kind word of encouragement or sympathy escapes the lips of those around Him. On the contrary, His persecutors, their expressions cold and heartless, continue to hurl abuses, their crude curses ricocheting off the surrounding stone walls in all their shameful blasphemy.

The centurions on horseback take over the rope-ends, reining in their prancing steeds to yank on the coarse twine tied around Christ's waist and around the crossbeam, in their callous efforts to raise His fallen body.

Even so, our contemplation of this Third Station must visualize Jesus rising from this, His first heavy fall, forcing Himself to an unsteady but upright position—the full weight of the crossbeam still resting across His torn and bleeding shoulders.

How often we ourselves have found the going rough—

Jesus Falls for the First Time
Strength

---

even been tempted to give up—especially during those times of weakness when we have fallen into sin and not had the temerity to admit our failings and to come before our Lord Jesus Christ, begging His forgiveness. We have only to meditate upon this, our Saviour's first fall along the *Way of the Cross*, to gain strength from His selfless determination in the face of immeasurable suffering and weakness to yet pick Himself up to continue on for our sakes.

O Most Sacred Heart of Jesus, we pray: Grant us the gift of Strength to lift ourselves up from despair born of our ugly sinfulness—to have faith in Thy loving forgiveness and to come before Thee on bended knee beseeching Thy mercy—with a renewed spirit of determination to amend our erroneous ways.

We adore Thee, O Christ, and we praise Thee
Because by Thy holy Cross Thou hast redeemed the world.

FOURTH STATION OF THE CROSS
Jesus Meets His Mother
Selflessness

The distance between the Prætorium and Calvary could not have been far, that portion of the Old City through which Jesus walked before exiting the last gate being estimated as a mere one-third of a square mile in area, and Golgotha simply stated in Sacred Scriptures as being close to Jerusalem.[1]

Not a great distance under normal circumstances, but every step an agonizing torture for the Son of Man in His weakened state. His body is wracked with pain as He staggers over the uneven cobblestones under the weight of the heavy crossbeam. Blood continues to flow in a steady stream down His beloved countenance. Wasps and flies persistently settle over its stickiness in spite of the sweep of the whip-lashes; Jesus unable to chase away their irritation with His hands still bound to the crossbeam.

We meditate on the great sacrifice Jesus is making for our sakes. In spite of the cruel and blasphemous behaviour of those around Him, He accepts their torments with patience and without complaint – continuing to offer up His sufferings to His Heavenly Father by way of atonement for our wretched

---
[1] John 19:20

sinfulness.[2]

Jesus Meets His Mother
Selflessness

After the point along the *Via Dolorosa* where Jesus falls for the first time, the street widens on its way to the exiting gate facing Calvary, still covered by cobbled paving and bound by thick stone walls, with the extreme heat of the day's sun bearing down through the gap above in all its intensity. The ugly mob builds up at this point, pinning themselves against the stone walls in their macabre mania to gloat over the suffering Victim as He passes by.

Our thoughts return to the Blessed Virgin Mary. She has left the stony alcove, and we can imagine her with John and Mary Magdalen moving quickly through the back streets of Jerusalem to come out into the main highway, thus getting caught up again with the vicious miscreants who had earlier been screaming for her Son's death by crucifixion. Together the three of them struggle against that wall of ferociousness, determined to reach Jesus.

In the near distance they can already make out the swaying weaponry of the Roman soldiers surrounding Jesus, the sun glistening off their metal armoury, their scarlet plumed helmets oscillating above the heads of the crowd. In trepidation we imagine the screams of demented souls continuing to resound about them.

Marching before the armed procession, and now coming

---

[2] Col.1:19-20

Jesus Meets His Mother
Selflessness

---

into view, is the trumpeter whose job it is to announce at regular intervals the sentence prescribed for the Prisoner, followed closely by the executioners carrying their implements of torture. As the Blessed Mother meets their cold gaze, how greatly her motherly heart suffers over the triumphant, callous glances they sling her way; for they would have been struck by her unique beauty, exuding an ethereal serenity and courage in spite of her clear distress, and it would have been passed around that this Woman was the Mother of the Nazarene. We can only imagine the wicked sneers of the executioners as they look upon that lowly *Mater Dolorosa*—no doubt in their supreme malice even shaking a nail or a hammer before her saintly countenance.

Closer creeps the procession until suddenly the soldiers give way to expose the Divine subject of their cruel ridicule—and in that agonized moment, the Blessed Virgin comes face to face with her Son Incarnate. Surely no words can describe the shocking horror of what Mary beholds: the bloodied, battered, bruised, beaten, scourged, scorned and violated figure of her beloved Jesus stooped under the heavy weight of that cumbersome Cross; His torn and bleeding hands helplessly bound to its crossbeam; His body shaking from inexorable pain. Her eyes quickly take in His sacred head crowned with that cruel ring of spiked thorns, blood raining down His bruised and lacerated face, His hair and beard stained red and matted in the heat of the morning sun. She painfully perceives those hideously open lacerations clearly visible where His dishevelled, blood-stained robe falls loosely off His shoulders; instantaneously, she notes His ripped and bleeding feet, the

Jesus Meets His Mother
Selflessness

---

cobbled stones wet from the flow of fresh blood. In shocked disbelief, the gentle Virgin reaches out to her Jesus, a mixture of horror and tortured empathy stamped across her gentle features.

And in that same moment we see the Son of God raise His blood-soaked head to look upon His Blessed Mother: His Most Sacred Heart equally pierced by a sword of unspeakable sorrow as He perceives and understands His Mother's grievous pain.

Yet in that brief exchange do we see the Son Incarnate console His agonized Mother, such a look of indescribable Love and Compassion emanating from that one Divine glance. Indeed we contemplate how the Son of Man, in these His lonely, scorned, humiliated and victimized moments, is similarly comforted by the presence of His devoted and loving Mother.

Immediately the guards close at hand give Jesus a shove, forcing Him forward, their ignorance, contempt and impatience having pushed them to the point of no return.

They dare not, however, touch the Mother of Christ, such being the Will of God that she be unharmed and inviolate. Gently John pulls her back from their threatening menace, his sturdy arms about the devastated *Mater Dolorosa*. We imagine her eyes fixed on Jesus, even as His frame is fast enveloped by the surrounding guards—now glimpsed intermittently and obscured by tears, flowing in abundance down Mary's lovely face.

Jesus Meets His Mother
Selflessness

But the effect of that Divine glance is not lost—for nothing can erase the gift of Christ's Comfort and Strength infused into the soul of His Blessed Mother. We ponder that moment, our hearts enthralled over the Selfless Love of our suffering Saviour. How like the Son of God to cross the divide of His own personal suffering to reach out and touch the devastated heart of His beloved Mother.

O Most Sacred Heart of Jesus, we pray: Grant us the gift of Selflessness—that, strengthened by Thy own example and that of Thy Blessed Mother, we may put aside our own misery and problems to reach out and help our fellowman, to empathize, comfort and console where needed.

We adore Thee, O Christ, and we praise Thee
Because by Thy holy Cross Thou hast redeemed the world.

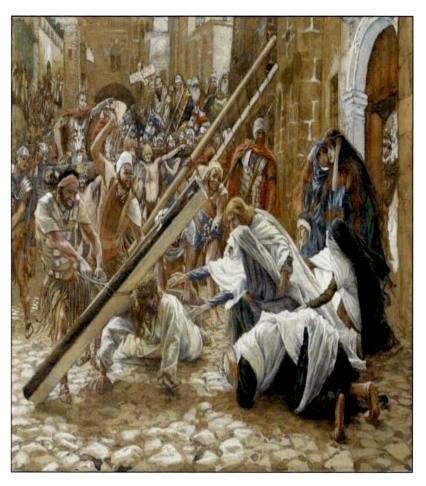

Jesus Meets His Mother

FIFTH STATION OF THE CROSS
Simon of Cyrene Helps Jesus to Carry His Cross
Faith

After the momentous and tragic meeting of Mother and Son, we can imagine Jesus continuing to be encouraged by the support of His beloved Mother as He senses her motherly presence along the Way of His sacrificial Cross. Just as the Blessed Virgin Mary, after looking into the eyes of her Divine Son, would be consoled and fortified to continue following His bloody Footsteps, all the way to Calvary.

We continue meditating on the Passion of Christ, logic dictating that the strength of our beloved Saviour must indeed be close to running out. Surely no man can continue under such dire circumstances. Already Jesus has lost sufficient blood to induce unconsciousness. Searing agony—dehydration—lack of food—lack of sleep—His body battered, bruised, beaten and scourged—all of which must inevitably bring the Son of Man to His knees. With great sorrowing we deliberate upon His weakened state as He staggers over the rough cobblestones of ancient Jerusalem toward the exiting gate, His knees shaking and close to collapse, His eyes fluttering from excruciating pain and extreme exhaustion.

It seems those enemies of Jesus accompanying the

Simon of Cyrene Helps Jesus to Carry His Cross
Faith

---

procession, predominantly the Pharisees and scribes,[1] in their macabre way fear for the Prisoner's failing strength—that He may not make it up the rugged heights of Golgotha to His Crucifixion. For at this Fifth Station along the *Via Dolorosa* we know a stranger in the crowd is called upon to help Jesus bear the weight of the heavy crossbeam—one named Simon of Cyrene.[2]

We reflect upon this moment in history. First, the stranger: undoubtedly a large man, perhaps used to hard labour by his appearance. Biblical Scriptures dictate he was from Cyrene, an ancient Greek colony in North Africa (now an archaeological site). It is conceivable that Simon was a black person or possibly Jewish, for during the reign of Ptolemy Soter (323-285 BC) some 100,000 Palestinian Jews settled in Cyrene. Mark 15:21 identifies Simon of Cyrene as the *father of Alexander and Rufus*, though no further explanation at this point as to who Alexander and Rufus might be. Perhaps, being in the company of their father, they were youngsters, which may account for Simon's initial reluctance to assist in the carrying of the Cross.[3] Or maybe Simon's reticence was simply born of fear—having witnessed the cruel treatment of the poor Man already sorely bloodied and clearly close to death, buckled under the weight of the crossbeam and struggling along the highway.

---

[1] Most likely the Sadducees, chief priests and elders would not have been present along the *Way of the Cross*.
[2] Luke 23:26; Matt.27:32
[3] Matt.27:32; Mark 15:21

Simon of Cyrene Helps Jesus to Carry His Cross
Faith

At the insistence of the Pharisees and scribes, the procession now pauses. They order that Jesus be cut free from the ropes binding Him to the patibulum. Two centurions on horseback approach. They rein in their restless steeds and stoop down to slash the coarse twine with their swords—their actions not quite synchronizing, causing Jesus to lose His balance and crash painfully to His knees on the uneven cobbled paving.

At the same time, two guards grab hold of Simon as he stands at the front of that closely-packed crowd lining the *Via Dolorosa*. His strong arms resist the arrest. A tussle ensues. The Pharisees and scribes remain close by, their cold eyes glinting insistence. More guards move in. The stranger from Cyrene has little choice. He is pushed roughly toward the fallen blood-soaked figure of Jesus.

At closer range, abject horror over the frightful state of the Man on the ground seizes hold of Simon. A sudden pity engulfs him.

Then does Jesus open His eyes. He looks up into the face of Simon; such a look of Divine Love. In an instance the man from Cyrene finds Faith. He stoops down offering his hand of assistance, tender compassion filling his eyes with emotional tears. Gently he helps Jesus to an unsteady but upright position.

Amid loud cursings—for the halt has created an irritating delay in the minds of the soldiers, anxious to reach Calvary—those on horseback once again pull on the rope ends to raise the heavy crossbeam from its position on the ground.

Simon of Cyrene Helps Jesus to Carry His Cross
Faith

Clumsily they drop the first portion of the patibulum over the shoulders of the strong Cyrenian, the remaining portion falling heavily on to the lacerated shoulders of our beloved Jesus.

Unbelievably, Simon now willingly embraces the Cross, his arms locked firmly around its coarse grain, determined to bear the greater portion of its horrendous weight. His eyes are fixed on Jesus at his side. His heart is filled with an inexplicable fascination for this Man of Galilee, meekly bearing His agonized torture without murmur or complaint. In shocked horror, he notes the cruel ring of thorns, his own body flinching at the sight of those razor-sharp needle-points buried deeply into the tender area across his companion's forehead; blood running in rivulets down His face and hair, gleaming in the morning's hot sunshine in all its copious ghastliness.

In spite of the hostile atmosphere surrounding the armed procession, a profound sense of Peace is settling over the man from Cyrene. An unfathomable Joy is lighting up his soul as he assists Jesus to carry the Cross.

"Take up My yoke" Christ promises His followers, *"for My yoke is sweet and My burden light"*.[4]

We marvel over the miraculous conversion of Simon. O Most Sacred Heart of Jesus, we pray: Grant that our own souls may become ever more enlightened by the gift of Thy holy Faith. May those who have lost their Faith, find it anew;

---

[4] Matt. 11:28-29

Simon of Cyrene Helps Jesus to Carry His Cross
Faith

---

and may those who have never experienced its sweet Consolation be inspired to look upon the Divine Countenance of Christ as did Simon of Cyrene, and find Faith.

*We adore Thee, O Christ, and we praise Thee
Because by Thy holy Cross Thou hast redeemed the world.*

SIXTH STATION OF THE CROSS
Veronica Wipes the Face of Jesus
Courage

Prior to the moment when Simon of Cyrene took upon his shoulders the Cross of our beloved Saviour, not having the rough burly guards on foot or the Roman centurions on horseback to pave their way along the *Way of the Cross*, we can imagine the Blessed Virgin Mary, shielded by the gentle giant John, with Mary Magdalen at their side, now overtaken by the hardiest of the pushing, shoving mob. They are joined by other followers of Jesus, among them the Blessed Virgin's own sister-in-law (Mary of Cleophas,[1] mother of James and Joseph,[2] brethren of Jesus)[3] and Salome (mother of John and James, the Sons of Zebedee),[4] each of them tearful, devastated and frightened.

Together they press forward, the plumed helmets of the centurions on horseback still visible ahead of them. Gratefully they have received word that the stranger from Cyrene is now helping Jesus to bear His Cross.

Indeed our thoughts return to Simon, every step of the

---

[1] Referred to by Matthew as "the other Mary" (Matt. 27:61; Matt. 28:1)
[2] Matt. 27:56; Mark 15:40
[3] Matt. 13:55, Mark 6:3, Acts 1:14 - James and Joseph, Jude and Simon referred to as brethren or brothers (i.e. near relations) of Jesus.
[4] Mark 15:40; Matt. 27:56; Mark 3:17

Veronica Wipes the Face of Jesus
Courage

---

way his heart surely touched by the diabolical suffering of his newfound companion Jesus—his soul whispering the profound Truth, that this Man could never be deserving of such maltreatment for only the purest of Love radiates from, through, and around His awesome Presence.

We reflect on the immense Joy that Simon's soul experiences the more he walks with Jesus. We can imagine his firm resolve to find out more about Him, knowing in his heart that this day will remain forever etched in his memory. Never again will his life be the same.

We can picture his eyes scanning the closely-knit mob for compassion, but only cruel, leering, mocking looks greet him along the Way—and the occasional backward frightened glance from those who are reluctantly caught up in the mob and eager to get away.

Then suddenly a woman appears. She has fearlessly stepped across the path of one of the horses at their side, causing the startled steed to rise up on back legs, almost overthrowing its rider. She hurls herself at the bleeding feet of the stooped-over figure of Jesus, sobbing incoherently. Before anyone can stop her, she stretches upward a lengthy veil of the finest weave in her hands—and quickly but tenderly blots the face of Jesus.[5]

---

[5] From the visions of Blessed Anne Emmerich, Augustinian nun, stigmatic, mystic, visionary, ecstatic. Sept. 8, 1774 - Feb. 9, 1824.

Veronica Wipes the Face of Jesus
Courage

Time stands still in that startling, unbelievable moment. The entire procession is brought to an abrupt halt before any one of the guards is stirred into action. They grab hold of the distraught woman and push her back into the crowd.

But the moment is not lost. For Simon—he is struck by the stupendous act of Courage and the brave Compassion with which the woman so determinedly blots the face of Jesus. His tear-filled eyes glance over the bloodied figure of his Companion, our own hearts enjoining Simon's in an overwhelming gratitude for the audacious act of this special lady.

We once again contemplate the Divine Countenance of Christ. We can imagine His eyes radiating a tender Gratitude as they follow the mystery woman being dragged from the scene.

In the meantime, both the Pharisees and the guards are greatly exasperated, not only by the sudden halt but much more by the public testimony of veneration paid to their Prisoner by the brave and compassionate act of the woman. At a look from the Pharisees, those guards close at hand commence striking and abusing our beloved Saviour with even greater force in their cruel effort to erase the impact of the moment.

Helpless to prevent their cruelty, and devastated over the continued vicious maltreatment of our Divine Redeemer, our thoughts return to the special lady. She has already disappeared through the crowd, clasping to her chest, the blood-stained veil. Tradition encourages us to meditate upon what became of this

Veronica Wipes the Face of Jesus
Courage

---

brave soldier of Christ and her prized possession.

On returning perhaps to the safety of her room, we can imagine her uncontrollable sobs as she grieves the torture of her beloved Jesus. Possibly family or friends take her into their arms, anxious to comfort her. Gently they pry the veil from her tight clutches to lay it over a nearby surface–only to become filled with absolute amazement at what they behold: stamped across its fine texture is the clear image of the Divine Countenance. Each and every one of them would surely have fallen to their knees as they stare incredulously at the wondrous miracle: the *vera icon* (true portrait) granted to His Faithful by our Lord and Saviour Jesus Christ.

Later, the lady to whom this precious gift was first bestowed became known as Veronica, and after her death, we believe the veil became known as The Veronica.

Even to this day, the veil is still treasured. It has been suggested that Veronica may have presented it to the Blessed Virgin Mary who kept it safe until her death, when it later passed into the safekeeping of the Apostles. In the year 700AD it was brought to Rome where, to this day, it remains preserved at the Vatican in St. Peter's Basilica, enshrined in the pier facing the high altar—before which stands a memorial statue to honour the Blessed Veronica.[6]

O Most Sacred Heart of Jesus, we pray: Grant us the gift

---

[6] Cruz 1984: 55-57

Veronica Wipes the Face of Jesus
Courage

---

of Courage, that we may never be afraid to stand up for what is good, righteous and just. Keep us strong against the forces of cowardliness, tempting us away from going out on a limb or standing outside of the crowd for Thy holy Name's sake.

We adore Thee, O Christ, and we praise Thee
Because by Thy holy Cross Thou hast redeemed the world.

The Icon Veronica

SEVENTH STATION OF THE CROSS
Jesus Falls the Second Time
Fortitude

How much Jesus appreciates every act of charity no matter how small on our part! We have only to look at Veronica to see how He lovingly rewarded her courageous act of charity with the Divine gift of His *vera icon*, and at Simon of Cyrene, upon whose soul He stamped the gift of Faith.

We ponder the rippled effect of those brave acts of kindness so richly rewarded: the image on Veronica's veil that brought comfort to the Faithful; Simon's conversion that helped to bring the Word of God to so many throughout his ensuing discipleship.[1]

Freshly inspired, we search for charitable ways through which we too can reach out to others, thereby comforting the Most Sacred Heart of Jesus in His great suffering: a suffering which endures down through the ages as mankind continues to offend His Infinite Goodness through our iniquities.

Inevitably our meditation returns to Christ's agony along the *Way of the Cross* that sorrowful Friday. Struggling

---

[1] Tradition dictates that Simon of Cyrene became one of the first early Christians.

Jesus Falls the Second Time
Fortitude

---

under the heat of the overhead sun, our weakening Jesus still stalwartly soldiers on, His body stooped and trembling, His knees threatening to crash Him to the stoned paving as they frequently buckle beneath Him. Even the large Simon of Cyrene is experiencing difficulty, his breathing laboured and coming in short gasps.

We picture the setting, our imagination enhanced by descriptive writings on ancient Jerusalem and the events kept in the hearts of Christ's devoted followers, relayed over the centuries and handed down by Tradition.

Thus inspired, we continue to meditatively follow Christ's bloody Footsteps, noting the surrounding thick stone walls built block upon heavy stone block, the blood of their innumerable harshly-treated slave labourers long since washed away by the tides of tim –the fresh Blood of Christ marking a new era of Freedom, Hope and Peace to all of His penitent Faithful. Over the years, since the time of Jesus, the level of the original *Via Dolorosa* has been raised by the accumulation of heavy silt deposits, thus blotting out all traces of His Most Precious Blood—erased, but never forgotten.

The erection of buildings too, has since altered the line of the streets, and at this Seventh Station, the old gate leading out of ancient Jerusalem directly to Golgotha has been walled up since the Middle Ages, the modern-day *Via Dolorosa* thus deviating at this point from the original route along which Jesus carried His Cross.

Jesus Falls the Second Time
Fortitude

We envision that walled-up gate and are suddenly besieged by returning thoughts to those biblical times: the gate now wide open, the air filled with the uproar of blasphemous shouting and the screams of demented souls surrounding Jesus; Simon of Cyrene at His side as together they shoulder the weight of the cumbersome crossbeam. We picture the approaching narrow vaulted archway at the entrance to the gate. A muddy pool lies stagnant at its base, replenished by the trickling water trapped overhead.

Slowly the constricted stone walls of the dank archway draw closer. Under the blistering sun, in His near state of collapse, we can imagine its mirage swaying before the dazed eyes of our beloved Saviour as He struggles to bring the image into focus, His mind reeling from absolute exhaustion.

A commotion ensues as the procession reaches the confines of the gloomy enclave, those on horseback having to draw forward or drop back. On entry, to our dismay, one of the guards on foot, irritated over their slow progress, gives Jesus an impatient shove.

Aghast, our meditation envisions Jesus instantly crumpling to His knees, falling face down in the foul-smelling waters of the muddy pool. At the same time Simon loses his balance, the crossbeam slipping from his shoulders and crashing heavily on to the inert figure of Jesus. Time for us stands frozen in that moment of absolute horror.

It takes Simon a second to rally from his own shock. He

Jesus Falls the Second Time
Fortitude

---

promptly laces his arms around the heavy beam and commences to pull on it, yelling frantically at the guards for assistance. Not out of their own willingness but simply a desire to rectify the delay, those close at hand take hold of the loose rope-ends attached to the crossbeam and for that brief period in time, many hands work to raise the cumbersome arms of the patibulum in the constricting confines of the archway. All too slowly, in our nightmarish meditation, the Cross is lifted off the motionless body of our beloved Saviour.

Yet again—unbelievably—our widening eyes must behold movement from under the bloodied, ripped garment; for history dictates that the Son of Man determinedly rises from this, His second major fall. Our contemplation witnesses His shoulders now hunching upward as first Jesus shakily draws up one knee and then the other, into an unsteady kneeling position. Immediately Simon reaches down to help Him upright. Surely the guards must be amazed—such Fortitude on the part of their Prisoner.

How many times have we given up, under far less onerous circumstances? How many times have we simply given up the fight to resist temptation and thus succumbed to its evil guiles? The longer we wait to admit our wrongdoing, the harder we find it to come back to God.

O Most Sacred Heart of Jesus, we pray: Grant us the gift of Fortitude—that we may rapidly rise up after falling into sin, to return to Thee with a spirit of true repentance and renewed

Jesus Falls the Second Time
Fortitude

---

determination to carefully avoid all occasions of sin—thus to never again offend Thine Infinite Goodness.

We adore Thee, O Christ, and we praise Thee
Because by Thy holy Cross Thou hast redeemed the world.

EIGHTH STATION OF THE CROSS
Jesus Meets the Women of Jerusalem
Consolation

Oh how distressing, the vision of our beloved Jesus after His fall into the slimy pool of water below the archway of the gate exiting Jerusalem. Dirty mud tracks now make their way down His Divine Countenance, drifting into His eyes to combine with a fresh flow of blood from the cruel ring of thorns, causing Him to flinch from their stinging effect as He painfully squints through half-shut eyelids to follow the trail at His feet.

Once past the gate exiting the city, the highway is crude and rough, pitted with uneven stones as it commences its gradual ascent up the rugged heights of Golgotha. We picture the feet of Christ, already bruised, cut and bleeding, and cringe over the additional pain and discomfort to our Divine Redeemer.

Overhead, the sun is a relentless ball of unprecedented fury, blazing forth from a cloudless blue sky. No hand of kindness reaches out to Jesus with water to slake His thirst, ease His parched throat, wet His cracked and bleeding lips. No shady tree casts a shield of cooling protection up that brief ascent. No gentle breeze brushes His burning brow.

We meditate on the slow progress of Jesus, His sacred body now stooped further forward, His faltering Footsteps more

Jesus Meets the Women of Jerusalem
Consolation

---

unsteady as He struggles under the burden of His sacrificial Cross, even with Simon of Cyrene bearing the greater portion of its cumbersome weight. In silent dread we follow Christ's bloody Footsteps, fearing the torturous fate fast looming ahead that awaits Him on Calvary's hilltop.

By now the remainder of the screaming miscreants have moved ahead, scrambling up the rugged slopes of Golgotha in their macabre eagerness to gain best vantage from which to view the imminent crucifixion.

But the Pharisees remain at hand, determined to ensure the Man from Galilee not escape, for they had heard how He mysteriously disappeared when His own townsmen had sought to throw Him over the cliffs of Nazareth.[1] Though sceptical, they feared His ability to perform wondrous deeds, having heard, and even witnessed, His healing of the sick,[2] the blind,[3] the dumb,[4] the lame,[5] even the lepers[6] and those possessed by demons;[7] how He had fed the five thousand on a mere five loaves and two fish,[8] and the four thousand with seven loaves and a handful of fish;[9] walked upon the waters, and calmed the

---

[1] Luke 4:29-30
[2] Luke 13:11-13; 14:2-4
[3] Luke 18:35-43
[4] Luke 11:14
[5] Matt. 9:2-7
[6] Luke 17:11-19
[7] Matt.4:24; Matt.8:33
[8] Luke 9:13-17
[9] Matt.15:36-37

Jesus Meets the Women of Jerusalem
Consolation

---

seas;[10] raised back to life the son of a widow woman in the city of Naim,[11] and the daughter of Jairus[12]—and Lazarus, brother of Martha and Mary, who had been dead in his grave for several days.[13] They monitor the procession closely, their eyes furtive and calculating, determined to ensure the Prisoner not get away.[14]

Perhaps the Roman guards on foot and centurions on horseback have similar fears, for they continue to circle Jesus as a vulture protecting their prey and those in charge of the rope-ends that bind our Saviour's body persist in yanking on them as though reining in an unruly charge on the verge of escape. We meditate on their insensitivity and find ourselves grieved by those occasions when we ourselves have lacked compassion, been cold-hearted, or unsympathetic.

Yet, surrounded as He is by such hostility, we can imagine the Son of Man continuing to be inwardly comforted by the presence of His loving Mother and that of His devoted followers,[15] sensing them close at hand as they follow in the wake of His bloody Footsteps.

Several of the other Holy Women, faithful disciples of Jesus who had witnessed His public miracles, rejoicing in the

---

[10] Matt.14:29
[11] Luke 7:12-15
[12] Luke 8:41-42, 49-55; Matt. 9, 1:38
[13] John 11:43-44
[14] Matt. 12:14; Mark 3:6; John 7:32
[15] John 19:25; Matt. 27:56

Jesus Meets the Women of Jerusalem
Consolation

---

wondrous gift of their Messiah (the living Christ),[16] are close behind, determined to keep up with the procession. With the lessening of the mob's density, they press closer, anxiously awaiting an opportunity to reach out to Jesus with compassion and kindness, so lacking in those keeping close watch over Him. They call out to their beloved Master.

Lifting His swollen, bloodshot eyes, Jesus turns to look at the weeping women as they move closer within His limited range of vision. Tenderly He addresses their tears, His soft words reaching out to their every ear just as His voice would carry across the hills, valleys and plains when He would address the people gathered in droves, eagerly attentive to His every word.

"Daughters of Jerusalem, weep not over me,"[17] He gently consoles them (it being His holy Will to thus suffer for our Redemption). His voice then filled with a great sadness, He somberly warns them: *"But weep for yourselves, and for your children. For behold, the days shall come, wherein they will say: Blessed are the barren, and the wombs that have not borne, and the paps that have not given suck. Then shall they begin to say to the mountains: Fall upon us; and to the hills: Cover us. For if in the green wood they do these things, what shall be done in the dry."*[18]

---

[16] John 1:41; John 4:25. Spelt as Messias in the Douay-Rheims text
[17] Luke 23:28
[18] Luke 23:28

Jesus Meets the Women of Jerusalem
Consolation

We contemplate these words of our Saviour. If, indeed, in the *green wood* of God's great love for us and our efforts to love Him in return, we can yet still become ensnared by life's many sinful temptations, how will we conquer our sinful passions if we become as *dry wood* with no Life within us.

We recall Christ's words to His apostles during His Last Supper with them when, like the *green wood*, He referred to Himself as a Living Vine—and are comforted by His clear instruction: *"I am the Vine: you the branches: he that abideth in Me, and I in him, the same beareth much fruit: for without Me you can do nothing."*[19]

O most Sacred Heart of Jesus, we pray: You taught the Holy Women of Jerusalem, and us too, to weep more over our own sinfulness rather than to grieve over Thy sufferings. May we be overcome with tears of remorse—and by renewing our Faith and growing in Virtue, grant that we may find Consolation in becoming living branches in Thee, the true Vine, thus bearing fruit for our Eternal Life.

We adore Thee, O Christ, and we praise Thee
Because by Thy holy Cross Thou hast redeemed the world.

---

[19] John 15:4-6

NINTH STATION OF THE CROSS
Jesus Falls a Third Time
Perseverance

It being the time of the Pasch, a number of travellers from nearby towns such as Bethlehem, Joppa, and Emmaus are heading for Jerusalem to celebrate the Feast. They inevitably come across the heavily-armed procession on its way to Calvary, its legion of steel-vested infantry and horse-ridden centurions in full regalia creating a terrifying presence in the narrow confines of the steep highway bound on the one side by the outer walls of Jerusalem, the other by the sloping Kidron Valley. In trepidation, the travellers press themselves against the stone walls to make way for the threatening force.

We can imagine their alarm over the savagely tortured Prisoner glimpsed within. They note how He struggles under the weight of the heavy crossbeam, assisted though He is by another (a rare occurrence to behold). Clearly the persecuted Prisoner is too weakened to carry the instrument of His execution alone. Their eyes take in His appalling condition— His blood-soaked garment—the ring of spiked branches crowning His bleeding head—the zealous maltreatment by His captors. Their ears pick up the coarse reviling aimed at the unfortunate Captive. Their curiosity is piqued yet mingled with more than a little fear as they carefully avoid catching the eye of any one of His vicious persecutors as they stomp by, their

Jesus Falls a Third Time
Perseverance

---

armoury making a loud clanking noise in the dry heat of the late morning sun.

Among the travellers are women with children. They pause in shocked disbelief at the unprecedented cruelty, hastily drawing their youngsters away from the frightful scene. Others are too stunned to move, a burning compassion instantly drawing tears to their eyes.

As the procession passes by, the troubled travellers now step aside for the disciples following closely in the wake of the procession. They stare at the obvious distress of the small group, noting their pale faces, drawn and tear-stained. Their attention is particularly caught by the beautiful woman at the forefront, her pallid countenance radiating a unique Serenity and Strength in spite of her clear distress; her eyes, red-rimmed from much weeping. Possibly some identify her as the Mother of the maltreated Prisoner.

We tearfully reflect on what the travellers behold: the unconscionable cruelty of the soldiers toward our beloved Jesus, already so cruelly battered, bruised, beaten, scourged, scorned and violated, staggering under the weight of His Cross toward Calvary with Simon of Cyrene assisting at His side.

As we follow Christ's faltering Footsteps we are reminded of another place and time. A time when those same forces of hatred, greed, fear and envy drove King Herod to seek out Jesus as a Child with the intent to kill Him, causing the

Jesus Falls a Third Time
Perseverance

Holy Family to flee into the safety of Egypt.[1] Now, ironically, those same forces, in calling for Christ's Crucifixion, assist Jesus the Man, through His redemptive suffering and ultimate Death on the Cross, to bring repentant souls (fleeing their own similar evil passions) into the safety of their Salvation.

Our thoughts return to the rugged slopes of Golgotha. We picture the hill, marked by alternating ridges and short plateaux, the arid vegetation growing more sparse with each increased elevation. We marvel at the Perseverance of our Saviour as He determinedly drags His failing body up the steep incline to meet His willed fate on Calvary's hilltop.

A short distance from the summit, Jesus suddenly falls—His third and final major fall. Like a nightmare in slow motion, our minds are tortured by the grim vision of His blood-soaked, pain-racked body now crumpling heavily to the ground; His weakened knees finally collapsing to dash Him against its stony surface.

Our imagination can scarce conceive Jesus finding sufficient strength to recover from the crippling effect of this final blow. We gaze upon His inert figure, each horror-filled second frozen in time.

With equal devastation, Simon of Cyrene looks helplessly down at Jesus, his eyes misting over with a fresh flow of tears, his attempt to reach down with a helping hand

---
[1] Matt. 2:13

Jesus Falls a Third Time
Perseverance

---

grossly hampered by the imbalance of the crossbeam. Even as he struggles to reach out to Jesus, several of the guards push him roughly away. They surround their Victim prostrate on the ground and commence kicking Him with their hob-nailed leather sandals; their harsh blasphemies clearly audible. We contemplate their relentless cruelty in the face of Christ's weakened state–and pray that we may never be found guilty of such callous insensitivity.

The sound of the trumpet breaks through our reflective desolation. The Roman commander now intervenes. Afraid that Jesus may not rally before Pilate's sentencing is carried out, he is putting a halt to the brutality. He barks orders to the surrounding soldiers to assist the Prisoner to a standing position. Slowly, painfully, Jesus rises.

We contemplate our Saviour's determined Perseverance as He now staggers forward to cover the remaining short distance to Calvary's summit, Simon in His wake, patiently bearing the full weight of the crossbeam out of love and respect for his new Master.

O Most Sacred Heart of Jesus, we pray: Grant us the gift of Perseverance that we may continue to press onward when the going gets rough—to never abandon our determined fight to overcome our sinful passions.

We adore Thee, O Christ, and we praise Thee
Because by Thy holy Cross Thou hast redeemed the world.

TENTH STATION OF THE CROSS
Jesus is Stripped of His Clothes
Chastity

Our hearts grievously torn over the great suffering and unfathomable lengths to which our Lord and Saviour is determined to undergo in order to make atonement to the Eternal Father for our sinfulness, we meditatively follow Christ's final Footsteps to Calvary's summit.

In growing fear, we reflect on the dreaded spot—'Place of the Skull' upon which Pilate's ignominious sentencing will culminate. The possessed demons of hate, pride, fear and envy already gathered—wolves anticipating the slaughter of the Sacrificial Lamb.

The precise location of Calvary[1] remains uncertain, as it no longer exists today. However, we know it to have been located outside the walls of ancient Jerusalem for Jewish law would not permit an execution (or burial) within the city's limits at that time. Its alleged hilltop, in the year 135AD was covered by a massive pavement under the reign of Emperor Hadrianus[2] (as a foundation for a pagan temple) and two centuries later, Constantine the Great,[3] first Christian Roman

---

[1] Matt. 27:33; Mark 15:22; John 19:17
[2] Roman Emperor Publius Aelius Hadrianus (76AD to 138AD)
[3] Emperor Flavius Valerius Aurelius Constantinus (272AD to 337AD)

Jesus is Stripped of His Clothes
Chastity

Emperor, ordered the paving removed and the first Church of the Holy Sepulchre built over the site. The vast structure still remains today, although its walls and facade have been changed many times over centuries of reconstruction to repair damage, desecration, and neglect. In fact, the Church of the Holy Sepulchre is now a magnificent edifice located within the walls of modern-day Jerusalem and is said to encompass not only the place of Christ's Crucifixion but also His sacred tomb (located as it was in the Garden close by[4]).

Certain descriptive writings and artwork depict Calvary's cavernous hillside as shapened not unlike a human skull (hence, as some believe, its name, 'Place of the Skull')[5] with its summit illustrated as a circular-shaped plateau broken by rough steps hewn out of the stony ground, the entire surrounds bound by a low stone wall bearing five openings by way of entrance. Ironically, five openings like the five wounds in the crucified body of our Saviour (His pierced hands, feet and side) through which flowed His Most Precious Blood, opening for us the Gates of Heaven.

We recall those occasions where the prophetic number *five* appears in Holy Scriptures: in the time of Moses, sacrificial peace offerings included five rams, five goats, and five lambs;[6] the Holy City (Jerusalem) had five gates (Gate of Ephraim, Dung Gate, Gate of the Fountain, Valley Gate and Corner

---

[4] John 19:41
[5] Matt. 27:33; Mark 15:22; John 19:17
[6] Numbers 7:17-83

Jesus is Stripped of His Clothes
Chastity

Gate); Probatica, the pond in Jerusalem known as the Pool of Bethsaida, had five porches in which lay the sick waiting for *the angel of the Lord to move the waters* to heal their infirmities.[7]

Indeed, Jesus often used the number *five* in His parables: the Parable of the Ten Virgins (five wise bridesmaids and five foolish ones);[8] the Parable of the Five Talents;[9] the Parable of the Supper wherein a man turned down the invitation for the sake of five oxen;[10] the Parable of the Two Debtors, the one who owed five hundred pence, the other fifty;[11] the Parable of the Rich Man who had five brethren;[12] the Parable of the Pounds wherein the second servant's pound with which the nobleman had entrusted him, gained five pounds in the nobleman's absence, gaining him power over five cities.[13]

In the discourse Jesus had with the Samaritan woman by Jacob's Well, He reminded her that she had had five husbands;[14] and in His teachings to the Apostles, Jesus chose five sparrows sold for two farthings[15] and warned of the households of five that would become divided, three against two, and two against three.[16] It was five thousand people whom

---

[7] John 5:2-4
[8] Matt.25:1-12
[9] Matt.25:14-30
[10] Luke 14:16 24
[11] Luke 7:41
[12] Luke 16:27
[13] Luke 19:18
[14] John 4:1 19
[15] Luke 12:6
[16] Luke 12:52

Jesus is Stripped of His Clothes
Chastity

Jesus fed on five barley loaves (and two fish).[17] Interestingly, too, Sacred Scriptures reveal that Elizabeth, wife of Zachary, after conceiving John the Baptist (born to herald the coming of Christ), hid herself for five months;[18] and the early Christians, after Christ's Resurrection were reported in the Acts of the Apostles as numbering five thousand.[19]

Our meditation returns to the busyness atop Golgotha. All five entrances are closely guarded by centurions on horseback. Hundreds of reinforcement soldiers are gathered in and around the area to ensure no untoward reaction from the unruly miscreants camped beyond the low stone wall. Moving to and fro among the crowd, the Pharisees, now joined by other of Christ's opponents, continue to fuel the wolves' lust for blood. A sense of doom pervades the area, mixed with solemn dread, fear–and demoniac rage.

We pause to consider the deep resentment and jealousy of those Pharisees and Sadducees, chief priests, ancients and scribes who opposed Christ's teachings and actions and who had sought to destroy our Lord and Saviour.[20] Throughout the Gospels we are reminded of certain of the Pharisees' self righteousness,[21] their hypocrisy,[22] and that of the scribes[23]—in

---

[17] John 6:1 13
[18] Luke 1:24
[19] Acts of the Apostles 4:4
[20] Matt. 12:14,.16:21, 20:18, 26:4; Mark 3:6; Luke 11:54
[21] Luke 18:10-14
[22] Matt. 5:20; Mark 12:38; Luke 11:43; Luke 20:46
[23] Luke 12:1; Luke 20:46-47; Matt. 23:13-29; Matt. 23:25-29

Jesus is Stripped of His Clothes
Chastity

---

claiming to love God yet behaving in a manner to indicate otherwise.

The Pharisees did believe that Jesus was the Messiah born of the line of David,[24] but did not believe Him to be Divine;[25] they, along with the scribes, believed He would be ruler over Israel—not a friend of Gentiles, publicans and sinners.[26] To their thinking, Jesus, in so doing, broke the law and by His healing of sins was guilty of blasphemy.[27] In fact, His very criticising them they considered to be an outrage.[28] The Sadducees in their turn opposed Christ's teaching on the Resurrection.[29]

"Generation of vipers, how will you flee from the judgment of hell?"[30] Jesus had warned the Pharisees and scribes;[31] as did John the Baptist similarly warn the Sadducees and the Pharisees.[32] We wince over the times we ourselves have behaved in a hypocritical or self-righteous manner.

In wide-eyed horror our contemplation now returns to the deep fissure in the rocky surface of Calvary's summit awaiting the erection of Christ's holy Cross; the vertical and its

---

[24] Matt. 22:41-45
[25] 1 Cor. 2:8
[26] Luke 7:34; Mark 2:16
[27] Mark 2:7
[28] Luke 6:6-11
[29] Matt. 22:23; Mark 12:18; Luke 20:27; Acts 23:8
[30] Matt. 23:33; Luke 3:7
[31] Matt. 23:1-29; Matt. 16:11; Matt. 6:2; Mark 7:6; Luke 12:56; Luke 13:15

Jesus is Stripped of His Clothes
Chastity

---

bloodied crossbeam lying alongside. Close at hand, one on the left and one on the right of the crevice, are the erected crosses of two criminals, their bodies already hanging pitifully from their gruesome mounts.[33]

We meditatively seek out Jesus. He is surrounded by the executioners, His body convulsing with pain and on the verge of collapse as He stands alone and silent before them; Simon of Cyrene prohibited by the soldiers from remaining with Him.

No eyes of pity greet our beloved Saviour, for those whose lot it is to prepare Him for crucifixion see not the Divine Son standing before them. Evil holds it own within their deadened souls, their hearts set as flint-stone. We see them as short thick-set men; inebriated, mocking grins fixed to their toothless, ferocious countenances.

Wasting no time, they proceed to strip the Divine Son of His garments with no thought but to humiliate their Victim— first savagely dragging His outer robe from His shoulders, then tearing away His undergarments with unflinching cruelty, determinedly ignorant of the extraneous pain inflicted upon our beloved Saviour; His body shuddering from shock as the brutal divestment rips open the wounds of His savagely scourged flesh. Their course reviling resound through the thin air. No compassion redeems their cold-heartedness. Nothing remits their blatant desire to debase the King of kings.

---

[32] Matt. 3:7
[33] Matt. 27:38; Mark 15:27; Luke 23:33; John 19:18

Jesus is Stripped of His Clothes
Chastity

We cringe over their heartless cruelty—yet must shamefully pause to reflect on those times we ourselves (albeit perhaps unwittingly) have debased the King of Kings through our own blasphemies and irreverence; all those times we have offended His Divine Majesty through our immodesty, lack of chastity, and acts of impurity.

Our thoughts return to the Virgin Mary, Mother Immaculate—to find her close by and now collapsed in the arms of John. How like the Almighty Father to engulf the consciousness of His pure and saintly daughter, thus sparing her the agony of watching her Divine Son so cruelly dethroned of His dignity before those contemptuous eyes of His sneering tormenters.

O Most Sacred Heart of Jesus, we pray: On account of all our sins of impurity, Thou didst permit Thyself to be stripped of Thy garments—to suffer such opprobrious nudity before those mocking onlookers. Grant that we may be determined to strip ourselves of all our impurities and vanities—in order to practice the holy Virtue of Chastity.

We adore Thee, O Christ, and we praise Thee
Because by Thy holy Cross Thou hast redeemed the world.

Calvary's Hill Top

ELEVENTH STATION OF THE CROSS
Jesus is Nailed to the Cross
Forgiveness

Roman crucifixions were abolished in 337AD by the Christian Emperor Constantine.[1] The ancient practice, employed as capital punishment by the Persians, Seleucids, Carthaginians, and Romans from around 6BC, was a particularly barbaric one, torturous in the extreme; its cruelty oftentimes exacerbated by the sadistic ingenuity of the executioner.

Typical with such crucifixions, the vertical of the cross would first be laid on the ground near the deep hole already prepared, awaiting the arrival of the prisoner who would be forced to carry the crossbeam to the place of crucifixion. The crossbeam would be nailed to the top end of the vertical with a piece of wood bound lower down to support the feet—and the upper body of the prisoner then transfixed to the crossbeam by heavy iron nails hammered through the hands or wrists, with the feet similarly nailed to the vertical. The entire cross would then be raised to an upright position and secured into the hole with stout stakes.

In exceptional cases, the vertical would already be staked into the ground before the crossbeam was nailed into place—and the prisoner would thus be nailed to the cross while in the standing position.

---

[1] Emperor Flavius Valerius Aurelius Constantinus (272AD to 337AD)

Jesus is Nailed to the Cross
Forgiveness

We shudder at the thought of such a heinous punishment. Medical literature on the subject further reveals that the fixed position of the victim's rib cage made it difficult to exhale and impossible to take in a full breath. As time passed, lack of oxygen and loss of blood would cause severe cramps, spasmodic contractions, and oftentimes unconsciousness prior to death.

In fearful horror we dread the fate that awaits our Divine Master. From the revelations of Saint Bridget of Sweden,[2] we believe His Crucifixion to have been as that outlined in exceptional cases; thus to have been a particularly cruel and painful one. Choking back sobs, we meditate on this Eleventh Station, our mind's eye scarce wishing to entertain its grim details.

With cringing reluctance we envision the stocky, thick-set executioners, their wild, inebriated expressions leering in malicious anticipation as they fix the vertical of the Cross into the deep crevice in the rocky surface of Calvary's hilltop, securing it at the base with stout stakes. Then they erected scaffolding with ladders leading up to a platform upon which they proceed to hammer into place the crossbeam of our Lord and Saviour Jesus Christ—already stained red from His Most Precious Drops of Blood.

We turn to the Blessed Virgin Mary. Her deathly-pale countenance is buried in the arms of John as he anxiously shields her from the shock of what is to come.

---

[2] Saint Bridget of Sweden (1303–July 23, 1373), mystic and canonized saint

Jesus is Nailed to the Cross
Forgiveness

Like a true lamb to the slaughter, the Sacrificial Lamb of God meekly ascends the rough ladder to the platform, clad in naught but a freshly girded loincloth, already soaking blood-red. Our shocked imagination envisions the ugly lacerations streaked across His entire body, the skin hanging in ribbons and exposing naked bone between the rivulets of freshly flowing blood.

Willingly, Jesus extends His arms. With shameless brutality, the executioners seize first His right hand (the hand that did so willingly bestow Divine favours) and savagely drive a thick, wrought iron stake into its sacred flesh—the first blow of their hammers instantly piercing the median nerve, causing a severe burning pain like lightning bolts traversing down the length of the arm of our beloved Saviour.

Yet impervious to the half-collapsed state of their shuddering Victim or to the jet-stream of fresh blood spattering their fiendish faces, those savage monsters seize hold of the other arm of our suffering Jesus, and screeching hideously, ruthlessly stretch it outward and upward, wrenching the bone from its socket[3] for the left hand to meet the opposing hole in the crossbeam, then hammering home another heavy spike into its sacred flesh.

Shamelessly insensitive to the extraneous, indescribable pain inflicted upon our beloved Saviour, like demented savages those insensitive demons, stretching His body beyond all bounds, similarly transfix Christ's feet to the Cross, thus

---

[3] Saint Bridget of Sweden (1303–July 23, 1373), mystic and canonized saint

Jesus is Nailed to the Cross
Forgiveness

---

rupturing the plantar nerve in each foot to cause further excruciating pain.

Can the atonement for our wretched sinfulness truly warrant such diabolical suffering?

Yet breaking through our shock and bewilderment—amazingly, unbelievably – our beloved Saviour, Son of God, is crying out to His Father in Heaven: *"Father, forgive them, for they know not what they do".*[4]

Our souls deeply mortified in the face of such unconditional Love, Compassion, and Mercy we crumple to our knees in trembling shame, deeply remorseful for ever having offended our Lord God's Infinite Goodness.

And yet the sadistic torturing is not over. With grim determination and mocking insults, those vicious executions then replace the crown of thorns (temporarily removed for the Crucifixion), hammering the sharp thorns into the sacred skull of our merciful Jesus, to bring forth a further abundant flow of His Most Precious Blood.

And now the Roman commander is ordering that the wooden plaque bearing Pilate's inscription be nailed to the top of the Cross. We wince over the persistent crash of iron on wood, the jarring further aggravating Christ's indescribable suffering.

---

[4] Luke 23:34

Jesus is Nailed to the Cross
Forgiveness

The Pharisees and Sadducees close at hand appear unaffected by the torture they are witnessing. Instead they angrily remonstrate over the exposed inscription reading *"Jesus of Nazareth, King of the Jews"*.[5] They are met by jeers from the Roman soldiers who point to their crucified King. Sheepishly they shuffle away, threatening to return to Pilate to have the sign altered. In fact, we know from Sacred Scriptures that some of the chief priests had earlier approached Pilate, demanding of him, *"Write not, The King of the Jews but that he said, I am the King of the Jews."*[6] Pilate, however, refused saying, *"What I have written, I have written"*.[7]

With reluctance, the masochists finally drop their implements and descend the roughly hewn ladders—mocking, self-satisfied smirks on their blood-spattered faces. They shift the scaffolding to one side and leave the scene, loping down the rugged slope like barbarous savages returning to their lairs.

A hush settles over Calvary's hilltop.

Already the pagan miscreants are turning away, apparently satisfied, while even the soldiers and guards and those who have witnessed the overly sadistic antics of the executioners are momentarily rendered speechless.

We contemplate this moment in history: the Son of God made Man, willingly suffering such unspeakable torture and the

---

[5] John 19:19; Matt. 27:37
[6] John 19:21
[7] John 19:22

Jesus is Nailed to the Cross
Forgiveness

---

ignominy of being hung from a tree—in atonement to the Eternal Father for our unconscionable sinfulness. In the Book of Galatians we read: *"Christ hath redeemed us from the curse of the law, being made a Curse for us: for it is written, cursed is every one that hangeth on a tree".*[8]

We recall the tree of forbidden fruit in the Garden of Eden[9] from whence the serpent's first temptation corrupted the world—and gaze upon this new tree of Life from which flows the streams of Christ's Most Precious Blood, purifying the world from the curse of sin.

O Most Sacred Heart of Jesus, we pray: Grant us the grace to crucify our own grudges and animosity toward others; to practice the virtue of Forgiveness toward one another as Thou dost so mercifully and generously Forgive us.

We adore Thee, O Christ, and we praise Thee
Because by Thy holy Cross Thou hast redeemed the world.

---

[8] Galatians 3:13
[9] Genesis 3:3

TWELFTH STATION OF THE CROSS
Jesus Dies on The Cross
Gratitude

Sacred Scriptures reveal that Jesus was crucified during the Third Hour[1] (around Noon on the modern day clock).

We contemplate Christ's excruciating agony. Blood runs in rivulets along the length of His suspended arms to trickle over His ripped and bleeding flesh, saturating the loincloth and continuing down His legs to join with the steady flow from His brutally pierced feet to collect in pools at the foot of the Cross. In gaping horror our meditation again envisions His flailed flesh, hanging in ribbons, exposing naked bone; not one portion of our beloved Saviour's body unviolated. Where not torn asunder by the savage scourging, His flesh is cut, bruised, and swollen from the frequent whiplashes, kicks, and punches.

As time draws on, Jesus struggles spasmodically to lift Himself in an effort to breathe through tortured lungs, His chest crushed by the weight of His suspended body. The very act forces the nails to tear the flesh further, as does the upward movement re-open the wounds on His lacerated back, causing blood to pour forth afresh into the already saturated grain of the Cross.

---

[1] Mark 15:25. Before the Third Hour had yet expired, when the Sixth Hour was close at hand.

Jesus Dies on The Cross
Gratitude

We selfishly turn to the Blessed Virgin Mary in search of motherly comfort. She is standing right there by her Divine Son at the foot of His Cross,[2] steadfastly never having abandoned Him (unlike we, who have so often forsaken our Lord God through our sinfulness). Her eyes, dark-circled and red-rimmed from much weeping, are fixed beseechingly on His Divine Countenance, her heart longing for His holy Will to put an end to His suffering.

In the words of Saint John Chrysostom:[3] *"Anyone who had been present then on* Mount *Calvary would have seen two altars on which two great sacrifices were being offered: the one in the body of Jesus; the other in the heart of Mary"*.

At her side remains John, devoted disciple, and close by are Mary of Cleophas (the Blessed Virgin's sister-in-law), Mary Magdalen, and Salome (mother of the Sons of Zebedee),[4] along with the other Holy Women. All of them courageously present though clearly frightened, distraught, and weeping. Each of them awaiting the fulfilment of God's holy Will in the deathly Sacrifice of the Paschal Lamb.

Others however, remain obstinately oblivious to the magnanimous majesty of God's saving love for the world. Among them we picture the small group of soldiers (described

---

[2] John 19:25
[3] Saint John Chrysostom (c.347-Sept.14, 407), Doctor of the Church, Archbishop of Constantinople
[4] Matt. 27:56; John 19:25

Jesus Dies on The Cross
Gratitude

---

by the Gospel writers John and Mark),[5] who loudly argue among themselves over the clothes, so cruelly stripped off the body of Jesus; the undergarments of which they have already torn into pieces and are dividing amongst themselves. The robe however, the one so lovingly woven for her Divine Son by the Blessed Virgin Mary, they have left intact and are now casting lots over it–thus in fulfillment of David's prophecy, *"They divided My garments among them; and upon My vesture they cast lots"*.[6]

Yet the blasphemous behaviour does not end here, for the remaining Pharisees, Sadducees, chief priests, scribes and ancients alike, passing by the foot of the Cross, wag their heads and call out in sneering tones, their blasphemies clearly audible to our Redeemer's sacred ears: *"Vah, thou that destroyest the temple of God, and in three days dost rebuild it: save thy own self. If thou be the Son of God, come down from the cross;"*[7] *"He saved others; himself he cannot save. If he be the king of Israel, let him now come down from the cross, and we will believe him;"*[8] *"He trusted in God; let Him now deliver him if He will have him; for he said: I am the Son of God."*[9]

How distressing their mocking insults. Our Divine Saviour treated as *a worm and no man: the reproach of men,*

---

[5] John 19:23-24; Mark 15:24
[6] Psalm 21:19
[7] Matt. 27-40
[8] Matt. 27:42
[9] Matt. 27:43

Jesus Dies on The Cross
Gratitude

---

the outcast of the people.[10] As prophesized in the Book of Psalms: *"all they who saw Me have laughed Me to scorn: they have spoken with the lips, and wagged the head."*[11] Even one of the criminals, crucified alongside of Jesus finds sufficient breath to cry out: *"If thou be Christ, save yourself and us."*[12]

How broken-hearted the Sweet Heart of Jesus over mankind's foolishness in not accepting His Infinitely merciful and saving Love. We look back to those times we ourselves have failed to appreciate the magnanimous gift of God's redemptive Sacrifice for our sake. We cringe over our lack of gratitude, and, even worse, like those scornful onlookers, have blasphemed our Lord and Saviour through our own careless choice of words.

Yet in that atmosphere of irreverence toward Jesus, *Son of the Most High*, we now hear the criminal hanging on the other side of Jesus, with a supreme effort rebuke the crucified thief: *"Dost thou not fear God seeing thou art condemned under the same condemnation? And we indeed justly, for we receive the due reward of our deeds; but this Man hath done no evil"*[13] and turning to Jesus, we hear his plea: *"Lord, remember me when Thou shalt come into Thy kingdom".*[14] We marvel over the words of this penitent sinner. Like Simon of Cyrene, he has

---

[10] Psalm 21:7
[11] Psalm 21:8
[12] Luke 23:39
[13] Luke 23:41
[14] Luke 23:42

Jesus Dies on The Cross
Gratitude

---

gazed upon the Son of God and suddenly found Faith.

With even greater wonderment, we once again ponder the compassionate mercy of our beloved Saviour in His prompt response: *"Amen I say to you, this day you will be with Me in Paradise"*.[15]

Overhead, the sun is a shrouded ball of blistering fury, the sky an opaque brilliance. In our mind's eye, we long to reach out with water to ease our Saviour's parched throat, soothe His cracked and bleeding lips, slake His aching thirst, wash away His weeping wounds endured for our iniquities. Oh that we could be resolved to make reparation for our iniquitousness through constant self-denial, self-sacrifice, and penance in loving Gratitude to our Redeemer.

As time drags on, a chilling air of desolation creeps over Calvary's hilltop. We can imagine the sun momentarily enshrouding itself under a pink fogginess as though reflecting the copious blood of Jesus poured out for the world.

Unexpectedly, a sudden darkness then descends.[16] An ominous darkness—one that not even the Pharisees or Sadducees can find a plausible explanation as to its cause. They glance nervously upwards. With silent nods to one another, they assemble together to make hasty tracks to leave. Many others are similarly fearful. Some are anxious to escape; others

---

[15] Luke 23:43
[16] Matt.27:45; Mark 15:33; Luke 23:44

Jesus Dies on The Cross
Gratitude

---

troubled and perplexed, gazing in stupefaction at the crucified figure of Jesus; perhaps remorse finding its way into their hitherto cold hearts.

As the darkness deepens, a biting wind whips up the Hill of Golgotha. The skies become troubled, lightening now flashing across the heavens in intermittent display, accompanied by muffled rumblings of thunder in the distance. Our meditation contemplates the Son of God, slumped further forward. His arms hang twisted and distorted from dislocated shoulders. We envision His Divine Countenance; His eyes continually look upward in prayerful union with the Eternal Father.

Now Jesus casts His eyes downward to look upon His grieving Mother as she stalwartly braces the wind, determined to remain at her Son's feet; His close friend and Apostle John by her side. His Most Sacred Heart filled with compassion, Jesus gently addresses His Mother, His voice clearly audible above the driving wind: *"Woman, Behold thy son!"*[17]

We ponder these four words clearly outlining the Incarnate Son's loving concern for His Mother to thus ensure that in her lonely widowed days she be taken care of by His faithful disciple John. We recall one other occasion reported in Holy Scriptures when Jesus addressed His Mother as *Woman* under a similar circumstance of expressed loving concern—at the Wedding Feast of Cana—after Mary, noting the failing

---

[17] John 19:26

Jesus Dies on The Cross
Gratitude

---

wine, had turned to her Divine Son out of compassion for the plight of the bride and groom. At that time Jesus, knowing such a public miracle would set into motion his Mother's great suffering, had gently responded, *"Woman, what is that to me and to thee? My hour is not yet come."*[18]

Breaking through our contemplation, again the voice of Jesus is heard above the driving wind and increasing bursts of thunder, *"Behold thy Mother!"*[19]

We are over-awed by these further words wrung from the crushed lungs of our beloved Saviour in these His dying moments. Surely Jesus had no need to expound upon the adopted mother-and-son relationship which His earlier words had implicitly implied. Indeed we note these three words are not qualified by the specific use of John's name. We pause then to reflect on their significance. Surely, logically, we must come to the conclusion that, having taken care of His Mother's need for a happy, secure home, Jesus now addresses the needs of all those who long to be called Children of God—by bequeathing to them His beloved Mother, this virtuous Virgin upon whom had been bestowed all Graces and from whom we can learn so much by simply following her saintly example, and begging her motherly assistance in our daily battle to avoid hurting Divinity's Infinite Goodness through our sinful passions and human weaknesses.

---

[18] John 2:4
[19] John 19:27

Jesus Dies on The Cross
Gratitude

For just as Mary had begged a favour of Jesus at the Wedding Feast of Cana, so equally will she gladly beg favours of Jesus on our behalf. *"Hail [Mary], full of Grace"*[20] the heavenly Angel Gabriel had greeted her; a beautiful and fitting greeting for us, too, to approach the Blessed Mother of the Word Incarnate. What could be more pleasing to our beloved Lord and Saviour than for us to acknowledge, respect and honour His beloved Mother by calling on her for motherly assistance.[21]

As the threatening storm gathers in momentum, we mourn our crucified Saviour. The intermittent flashes of lightening outline His fallen head crowned with that cruel ring of thorns—His scourged and ravaged body lit up in grim detail by the ghostly lighting, His holy Cross swaying under the pull of the howling wind.

Our thoughts return to the Book of Psalms, our Redeemer's terrible agony so accurately prophesized by David: *"Many calves have surrounded Me: fat bulls have besieged Me. They have opened their mouths against Me, as a lion ravening and roaring. I am poured out like water; and all My bones are scattered. My heart is become like wax melting in the midst of*

---

[20] Luke 1:28
[21] Saint Thomas Aquinas, O.P. (1225 – 7 March 1274)
   Italian priest of the Catholic Church in the Dominican Order, immensely influential philosopher and theologian in the tradition of scholasticism; known as Doctor Angelicus (the Angelic Doctor) and Doctor Communis or Doctor Universalis (the Common or Universal Doctor).

Jesus Dies on The Cross
Gratitude

My bowels. My strength is dried up like a potsherd, and My tongue hath cleaved to My jaws: and thou hast brought Me down into the dust of death. For many dogs have encompassed Me: the council of the malignant hath besieged Me. They have dug My hands and feet. They have numbered all My bones. And they have looked and stared upon Me".[22]

About the Ninth Hour,[23] alone in His humiliation and torment as the Son of Man's redemptive mission on earth reaches its climax, His agonized cry suddenly breaks through the stormy wretchedness, "*Eloi, Eloi, lamma sabacthani?*" (*My God, My God, why hast Thou forsaken me?*).[24]

Such heart-stopping words from our tortured Redeemer! What chilling a realization for our own souls—the hideousness of our pride, covetousness, lust, anger, gluttony, envy, slothfulness, blasphemy, obscenities, in fact all our evil and uncharitable ways in the sight of the Eternal Father—such that His Divine Majesty must turn away, so great is His hurt and disgust. Choked by sobs of wretched misery and shame, we determine even more to never again to offend His Infinite

Goodness—the pain of losing our God wringing from our own hearts, the devastating words of our Saviour, "*Eloi, Eloi, lamma sabacthani?*".

---

[22] Psalm 21:13-18
[23] The biblical Ninth Hour being from 3:00 pm to 6:00 pm
[24] Mark 15:34; Matt. 27:46

Jesus Dies on The Cross
Gratitude

Sacred Scriptures confirm that Jesus *knowing all things were now accomplished*[25] then cried out: *"I thirst"*.[26] A centurion standing by hastily soaks a sponge in vinegar from a vessel on hand, and spearing it now rushes forward, shoving the sponge roughly into the lacerated and bleeding mouth of our Redeemer.[27] Having sought not to ease His discomfort or quench His thirst throughout His entire Passion,[28] we are compelled to conclude that these words were not a quest for liquid but more Christ's thirst for those souls who would be lost in spite of this, His absolute redemptive Sacrifice.

No doubt these words would have similarly grieved His Blessed Mother; her own heart, enjoined as it was to that of the Incarnate Word from the moment of her willing *Fiat* to God's plan of Salvation for the world.[29]

As Saint Augustine[30] poignantly states: *"When Jesus said these words, He was looking for Faith from His own people but because He came unto His own, and His own*

---

[25] John 19:28
[26] John 19:28
[27] John 19:29
[28] Matt. 27:34; Mark 15:23
[29] Luke 1:38
[30] Augustine of Hippo (November 13, 354 – August 28, 430), Bishop of Hippo Regius, also known as St. Augustine or St. Austin, philosopher and theologian; Latin church father, claimed as one of the most important figures in the development of Western Christianity.

Jesus Dies on The Cross
Gratitude

---

received Him not,[31] instead *of a sweetness of Faith, they gave Him a vinegar of faithlessness."* In the words of Leo the Great,[32] *"Having now tasted the vinegar, produce of the vineyard that had degenerated in spite of its Divine Planter"* Jesus then breathed His last—His dying words borne across Calvary's desolate hilltop: "*Father, it is consummated.*[33] *Into Thy hands I commend My spirit*".[34]

It is finally over.

In the Temple of Jerusalem, the curtain separating the Holy of Holies from the rest of the sanctuary, symbolically separating the dwelling place of God from man, is torn from top to bottom its entire length.[35] Further, the Gospel writer Matthew records that *the earth quaked and rocks were rent.*[36]

On the Hill of Golgotha, fear holds its own. Many flee the scene, striking their breasts and wailing[37]—while at least one Roman centurion falls to his knees, crying out incredulously, "*Indeed this was a Just Man.*"[38]

---

[31] John 1:11
[32] Pope St. Leo I (the Great), reigned 440-61, place and date of birth unknown, died 10 November, 461. Leo's pontificate, next to that of St. Gregory I, is the most significant and important in Christian antiquity.
[33] John 19:30
[34] Luke 23:46
[35] Mark 15:38; Matt. 27:51
[36] Matt. 27:51
[37] Luke 23:48
[38] Luke 23:47

Jesus Dies on The Cross
Gratitude

Grief-stricken yet undeterred, at the feet of her Son remains the Blessed Virgin Mary, now in the arms of her adopted son John. Mary of Cleophas, Mary Magdalen, and Salome stand at a respectful distance close by, equally devastated and weeping.

We contemplate the Virgin Mother's great grieving at this point, her body wracked with sobs as she mourns the death of her Jesus—God's only Begotten Son made Man, born into the world as the Pascal Sacrificial Lamb to suffer and die in atonement to the Eternal Father for our wretched sinfulness. The redemptive work of her Son Incarnate now over, how Mary's lonely motherly heart would be longing to be enjoined with that of her beloved Son.

"I am the Good Shepherd. The Good Shepherd giveth His life for His sheep"[39] Jesus had told His disciples—and on another occasion He had compounded His great love for us by saying, *"No greater love is this than a Man lays down His life for His friends"*.[40]

O Most Merciful, Loving and Compassionate Saviour, we give Thee thanks for Thy great love for us. *Wounded for our iniquities*[41] Thou didst endure abominable sufferings throughout Thy Passion and Crucifixion to atone for our countless sins, offenses and negligences toward the Eternal Father. Never again

---

[39] John 10:11
[40] John 15:13
[41] Isaiah 53:5

Jesus Dies on The Cross
Gratitude

---

will we forget our Gratitude!

    O Most Sacred Heart of Jesus, we pray: May we grow ever more Grateful as we contemplate the great Mysteries of our Redemption—and learn to express our appreciation by endeavouring to live our lives free from sin. May we also resist complaining in favour of gratefully counting our many blessings which Thou dost lavish so generously and mercifully upon each and every one of us sinners.

*We adore Thee, O Christ, and we praise Thee
Because by Thy holy Cross Thou hast redeemed the world.*

Statue of Our Lady of Sorrows, located between the Catholic (right) and Greek (left) chapels of Calvary. This is Station 13 on the Via Dolorosa, at which Mary receives the body of Jesus from the cross

THIRTEENTH STATION OF THE CROSS
The Body of Jesus Is Taken Down From The Cross
Repentance

In spite of the early afternoon hour, believed to be within the Ninth Hour[1] (some time after 3:00 pm on the modern clock), the blackened skies persist, enshrouding Calvary's hilltop—broken only by the brilliant bursts of lightening.

In the mournful desolation, shattered spasmodically by the increasing peals of thunder, the howling wind moans across its desolate plateau like a mighty dirge, tugging mercilessly at the lifeless body of our Lord and Saviour as He hangs limply from His saving Cross. Choking back sobs of tearful remorse, we picture the sacred head of Jesus bowed in submission to the Eternal Father; the cruel ring of thorns now a painless crown of glory bathed in the intermittent ghostly lighting.

All those whose malice, jealousy, fear, and greed had spurred on Christ's ignominious Crucifixion, have fled the scene, terror giving wings to their flight in the onslaught of the inexplicably troubled and menacing elements.

Only the Blessed Virgin Mary with John by her side maintain their sorrowful vigil at the feet of Jesus, while at a short respectful distance from the Cross, the group of Holy

---

[1] Matt. 27:46; Mark 15:34; Luke 23:44-45

The Body of Jesus is Taken Down from The Cross
Repentance

Women[2] and other faithful disciples remain huddled together, the women sobbing quietly.

It being the Parasceve of the Pasch (the eve of the Sabbath),[3] under Rabbinical Law the Sabbath day was not to be defiled nor the people defiled by touching the dead. Certain of the Jews therefore not wishing the bodies to remain on the crosses after sunset (the beginning of the Sabbath), request of Pilate that the legs of the crucified victims be broken, in order to put an end to their lives and ensure their burial before the commencement of the Sabbath.[4] Pilate immediately dispatches executioners to Calvary to carry out their wishes.

Arriving at the scene, the soldiers first smash the legs of the two criminals[5] crucified one on either side of our beloved Saviour. They then turn to the body of Jesus. A sudden flash from the heavens lights up His lifeless gaze, negating the need to break His sacred knees:[6] thus in fulfilment of Holy Scriptures, *"You shall not break a bone of Him"*.[7]

Instead, in order to confirm death one of the soldiers thrusts his lance into the side of Jesus,[8] burying its spearhead deep into the sacred flesh (once again in fulfilment of Holy

---

[2] Mark 15:40
[3] Mark 15:42; John 19:31
[4] John 19:31
[5] John 19:32
[6] John 19:33
[7] John 19:36
[8] John 19:33

The Body of Jesus is Taken Down from The Cross
Repentance

Scriptures, *"They shall look upon Him whom they pierced"*).[9]

In abject horror, we can imagine the look on the face of the Blessed Virgin Mary and on that of John—time held for a moment in a capsule of heart-wrenching disbelief.

Even as we envision their shocked dismay, as the spearhead is withdrawn, yet another flash of lightening reveals flowing forth from the single open wound in Christ's side, two distinct streams—one of blood, the other of water![10]

John later wrote in his Gospel: *"He that saw it hath given testimony, and his testimony is true; he knoweth that he saith true, that you also may believe"*,[11] and as we read in the First Epistle of Saint John: *"This is the One who came by water and blood, Jesus Christ"*.[12] The Roman centurion, his lance thrown aside, crumples to the ground in incredulous wonder, moaning sorrowfully, *"Indeed this was the Son of God"*.[13]

As we marvel over this amazing phenomenon, the ultimate outpouring of the Sacrificial Blood of our Redeemer coupled with the stream of Living Waters flowing from His side, we remember the words of Zacharias' prophecy: *"On that day a Fountain shall be opened for the House of David and the inhabitants of Jerusalem, to cleanse them from sin and*

---

[9] John 19:36-37
[10] John 19:34
[11] John 19:35
[12] I John 5:6
[13] Matt. 27:54; Mark 15:39

The Body of Jesus is Taken Down from The Cross
Repentance

---

impurity";[14] later explained by Bishop Fulton J. Sheen:[15] *"The arrow of sin that wounds and crucifies brings the balm of Forgiveness that heals"*.

Even as our meditation draws tears of incredulous wonder over this miracle, so do the angry skies now release their own voluminous teardrops, dropping in straight curtains of water—promptly drowning the earth in teaming rivulets and swallowing up the Most Precious Blood of our Saviour.

Gently John shepherds the devastated *Mater Dolorosa* to a nearby cavern, there to protect her from the weeping heavens, wherein her sister-in-law (Mary of Cleophas), Mary Magdalen, Salome (mother of the Sons of Zebedee),[16] and others of the Holy Women and devoted disciples are there to share in her immense grieving.

Back in Jerusalem, Joseph of Arimathea, secret disciple of Jesus,[17] and Nicodemus, ruler of the Jews,[18] boldly seek an audience with Pilate to gain his permission to take down the body of Jesus. They now appear at the entrance of the cavern, Joseph armed with fresh linen cloths, Nicodemus with a mixture of myrrh and aloes, about a hundred pound in weight for the

---

[14] Zach.13:1
[15] Born Peter John Sheen (May 8, 1895–December 9, 1979), American Bishop of the Roman Catholic Church. His cause for canonization for sainthood was officially opened in 2002.
[16] John 19:25; Matt.27:56
[17] John 19:38, Luke 23:51; Mark 15:43; Matt.27:57
[18] John 3:1-9

The Body of Jesus is Taken Down from The Cross
Repentance

---

burial.[19]

Finally, the skies having spent their tearful energy, the sorrowful Mother, surrounded by John, the Holy Women and other disciples, leave the grotto to make their way back to the holy Cross and the lifeless body of their Beloved.

With the gentlest of care and reverence, they take down the body of Jesus, wrapping Him in the fresh linen cloths; then tenderly place Him in the waiting arms of His Mother. How much Mary would have longed to hold her Son, comfort and console Him throughout the gruelling ordeal of His terrible Passion.

Our meditation encompasses that sorrowful scene; the devoted followers of Jesus surrounding the weeping *Mother of Sorrows*, their tears enjoining hers to flow over the lifeless body of our beloved Saviour. Surely no words can describe their great sorrowing, especially that of the Virgin Mary, who, by her willing *Fiat* to the Angel of God that holy night of the Annunciation, humbly undertook to partake in the redemptive Sacrifice of the Word Incarnate in order to save the world.[20]

In the dim lighting of that late afternoon, we envision the wounds of our beloved Saviour, washed clean by the might of the heavenly downpour:

---

[19] John 19:39
[20] Luke 1:38

The Body of Jesus is Taken Down from The Cross
Repentance

➤ His sacred body—so savagely scourged on account of all those times we have lashed out at one another in anger, spite, jealousy, hatred and vengeance.

➤ His head—so cruelly crowned on account of all our sins of pride and arrogance, our covetousness and manipulative scheming, our lustful thoughts and unrestrained passions, our sacrilege and blasphemies, our profanities and abusive behaviours. Our stubborn determination to turn a deaf ear to the Word of God.

➤ His hands—so brutally nailed to the Cross on account of all our negligent, dishonest, and lazy ways, our sinful habits and evil works, our sins of self-gratification and gluttony, our frivolous waste of time and energies.

➤ His feet—so savagely pierced on account of all those times we have ignored His holy Will and gone our own impulsive and erroneous ways.

➤ His Most Sacred Heart—so viciously pierced on account of our cold-heartedness, insensitivity, and multitudinous sins against charity.

Cringing in shame, we fall on our knees, our own tears flowing in abundance over the crucified body of our Divine Redeemer.

O Most Merciful Heart of Jesus, we pray: Grant us the

The Body of Jesus is Taken Down from The Cross
Repentance

---

gift of true Repentance that we may be filled with genuine remorse for ever having offended Thee. May we be determined to make amends through a humble confession followed by a diligent penance–and by the help of Thy Grace, may we strive ever more determinedly to never again offend Thine Infinite Goodness through our sinful, negligent, careless, and hurtful ways.

We adore Thee, O Christ, and we praise Thee
Because by Thy holy Cross Thou hast redeemed the world.

THE BURIAL OF CHRIST
Now in the place where he was crucified there was a garden; and in the garden a new sepulchre, wherein was never man yet laid. (John 19: 41)

FOURTEENTH STATION OF THE CROSS
Jesus is Laid in the Tomb
Hope

At this Fourteenth Station of the Cross, we pause to consider Nicodemus and Joseph of Arimathea, both prominent men at the burial of Jesus.

Nicodemus was a Pharisee,[1] an elderly ruler of the Jews,[2] a master in the community and a member of the Sanhedrin.[3] He came to Jesus at night, saying *"Rabbi, we know that Thou art come as a teacher from God, for no man can do these signs which Thou dost, unless God be with Him."*[4] And in response to his eager questioning, Jesus revealed, *"God so loved the world as to give His only Begotten Son; that whosoever believeth in Him may not perish, but may have Life Everlasting. For God sent not His Son into the world to judge the world, but that the world may be saved by Him"*.[5]

Joseph of Arimathea was reputed to be a rich man,[6] a noble counsellor,[7] a member of the Sanhedrin.[8] He too had been

---

[1] John 7:50
[2] John 3:1
[3] Jewish Judicial Council
[4] John 3:2
[5] John 3:16-17
[6] Matt.27:57
[7] Mark 15:43
[8] Luke 23:51

Jesus is Laid in the Tomb
Hope

---

searching for the Truth, and having found it in Jesus, became a secret disciple of our Lord (for fear of repercussion from the Jewish leaders).[9] Being a man of substance, he owned a tomb in the Garden close to where Jesus was crucified; a sepulchre never used before.[10] It was to this tomb that he directs the Blessed Virgin Mary and her Son's devoted followers that mournful Eve of the Pasch.

How providential that it should be a Joseph (this devout man of the House of Arimathea)[11] who offers shelter for the lifeless body of Jesus; just as it was a Joseph (most chaste spouse of the Virgin Mary, devout man of the House of David)[12] who sheltered Jesus during His lifetime. And just as Joseph (espoused to Mary, carrying the holy Christ Child in her virgin womb)[13] placed his complete trust in God to protect him and his betrothed from wagging tongues, so too does Joseph of Arimathea now place his complete trust in God to protect him from the Jewish leaders, determined as he is to give His Master a dignified burial.

How fitting that the King of Kings, though *with the wicked He was reputed*[14]—indeed, tried as a criminal and crucified between two thieves[15]—be buried in the new and

---

[9] John 19:38
[10] John 19:41;
[11] Luke 23:50
[12] Matt.11:19
[13] Matt. 18-20
[14] Mark 15:28
[15] Matt. 27:38; Mark 15:27; Luke 23:32; John 19:18

Jesus is Laid in the Tomb
Hope

---

undefiled grave of a noble and honourable man.[16]

Our thoughts return to the *Mater Dolorosa* and other mourners of our Redeemer; each of them courageous and steadfast to the end in spite of the surrounding demons and the ugly mood of Christ's cruel oppressors all along the *Way of the Cross,* culminating here on Calvary. Together with Joseph of Arimathea and Nicodemus, they cross the dimly lit, desolate hilltop, tenderly carrying the body of Jesus to the sepulchre in the nearby Garden–there to carefully negotiate the stone steps[17] into the depths of its candle-lit crypt.

In humble reverence, they help the Blessed Mother to prepare the sacred body of her Jesus for burial in accordance with Jewish custom, each of them choking back silent sobs as they mourn the death of their Beloved.

The initial preparations finally complete, we can imagine the sorrowful group one by one taking their departure, extinguishing the candles before exiting—to leave a single lit candle, perhaps with John, as he alone remains behind with the weeping Virgin Mary.

Our hearts can scarce entertain the devastation of that gentle Mother, her soul grievously pierced by a sword[18] as prophesized by Simeon at the Presentation of her baby Jesus in

---

[16] Isaiah 53:9
[17] Luke 23:53; Matt. 27:60; Mark 15:46
[18] Luke 2:35

Jesus is Laid in the Tomb
Hope

---

the Temple of Jerusalem all those years ago. We trace her silent tears, flowing in abundance down her beautiful face, her dark luminous eyes filled with an immeasurable depth of sadness.

We picture her looking down at the linen cloths enshrouding the lifeless body of her Jesus, then turning her tearful gaze to His Divine Countenance, ghostly grey in the dim lighting and barely recognizable under all its savage lacerations and bruising. Choking back sobs, with sweet motherly tenderness, Mary stoops now to kiss the brow of her beloved Son in a final gesture of farewell before we see her tenderly cover His Holy Face with a small white linen cloth.

Gently John shepherds the weeping *Mother of Sorrows* out into the bleakness of the late afternoon, there to be surrounded by Mary of Cleophas, Mary Magdalen, Salome, and the other Holy Women. With sombre reverence, the men folk roll a large stone across the entrance of the sacred tomb[19]—final resting place of our Lord and Saviour Jesus Christ.

We can imagine John guiding the sorrowing Virgin, surrounded by the others, back through the Garden; their senses too numbed by grief to appreciate its sweet fragrances of almond, olive, and pine wafting through the late afternoon air, eve of the Pasch.

They return to Jerusalem, grief-stricken and devastated—yet strong in the face of the Divine promise that

---

[19] Matt. 27:66; Mark 15:46

Jesus is Laid in the Tomb
Hope

---

they would see their Beloved again on the third day.

"*As Jonas was in the whale's belly three days and three nights: so shall the Son of Man be in the heart of the earth three days and three nights*"[20] Jesus had told the Pharisees and the scribes during one of the many occasions they (and the Sadducees) had tried to trip Him up with their devious questioning. And on another, in their presence He had told the Jewish people in the Temple of Jerusalem, "*Destroy this Temple, and in three days I will* raise *It up.*"[21] We know He was referring to the Temple of His sacred Body but the Pharisees, Sadducees and scribes stubbornly refused to see the light of Christ's words—though they had heard sufficient to make them wonder.

They now approach Pilate, saying: "*Sir, we have remembered that that seducer said, while he was yet alive: 'After three days I will rise again'. Command therefore the sepulchre be guarded until the third day lest perhaps his disciples come and steal him away,* and *say to the people: 'He is risen from the dead' - for the last error shall be worse than the first.*"[22] Matthew's Gospel confirms that Pilate then said to them, "*You have a guard; go, guard it as you know*" and that *they departing, made the sepulchre sure, sealing the stone, and*

---

[20] Matt. 12:40
[21] John 2:19
[22] Matt. 27:63-65

Jesus is Laid in the Tomb
Hope

---

setting guards[23] over it.

But there is nothing the Pharisees, the Sadducees, and the scribes can do to thwart the Divine Plan. We know that on the third day, Easter Sunday, Jesus did indeed rise from the dead[24] –His resurrected body clothed in immortality and glory, one that could appear and disappear, go through material objects, ascend to and descend from Heaven.[25]

We ponder the significance of this Glorious Mystery of Christ's Resurrection, completing the mystery of our Redemption and Salvation.

"For when you were the servants of sin, you were free men to justice. What fruit therefore had you then in those things of which you are now ashamed? For the end of them is death,"[26] wrote Saint Paul to the Romans. *"But now being made free from sin, and become servants to God, you have your fruit unto sanctification, and the end, Life Everlasting."*[27] Precious Gift indeed: as further expounded by Saint Paul—for while *the wages of sin is death,*[28] the reward of repentance is Life Everlasting[29] and the Unsurpassed Joy of our Eternal Salvation!

---

[23] Matt. 27:66
[24] Matt. 28:6; Mark 16:6; Luke 24:6-7; John 20:19
[25] John 3:13; Eph. 4:10; Proverbs 30:4-5;
[26] Romans 6:20-21
[27] Romans 6:22
[28] Romans 6:23
[29] Romans 4:25; 6:23

Jesus is Laid in the Tomb
Hope

Sweet promise of Christ to each of His penitent Faithful–wondrous ray of Hope that shines through every darkness, purchased for us by our Saviour's sacrificial Passion, Crucifixion, Death and Resurrection.

O Most Sacred Heart of Jesus, fount of Love and Mercy, teach us to bury all our *sinful* passions—to *love one another*[30] as Thou hast loved us—that we may live our lives in a manner befitting to Thy sweet promise—Hope of our Eternal Salvation; thus to arise to a new life in the Kingdom of Heaven with Thee, our Divine Lord, Master and King—wherein all our *sorrow shall be turned into joy*[31] and the *Peace of God, which surpasseth all understanding*[32] shall abide within us for ever.

We adore Thee, O Christ, and we praise Thee
Because by Thy holy Cross Thou hast redeemed the world

---

[30] John 13:34; John 15:12
[31] John 16:20
[32] Phil. 4:7